Empathy Road

Charles Goldman

Table of Contents

Empathy Road...1

I..1

II...3

III..5

IV..7

V..8

VI...9

VII..10

VIII...11

IX..13

Offal Sings the Wheel...17

If Electricity Doesn't Crackle...18

Who Comes in That Hour of Darkness?.....................................19

Once in a Dream I Saw a Man..20

While the Chimes Which Mother Bought...................................21

January Third...22

The Root of the Flower of the Sky...24

Caterpillar and Snake...25

The Task Which Must Be Mastered...26

If Only...27

In the Real Forever..28

I..28

II...29

III..30

IV..31

My House and My Rock...33

Live in This Willowy Land..34

Woman as Star...35

The Rock which Holds Us..36

The Chess of Blood 38

If I Could Write the Breeze 39

Do Not Follow Me.. 41

In the Bright Golden Chill of Morning................................ 43

The Ring and the Flesh 44

The Empty Plaza... 47

A Beggar's Song 49

The Red Woman.. 50

Out of the Emptiness Arising 52

The First Stone 53

Bring Only Beauty.. 55

That Strange and Seamless Sky 56

Clinging 57

I Walk Among the Comets 58

Dead Ode 59

Plain and Hollow 60

The Screaming and Screeching Sky of Her Ecstasy 62

Whole City Limping... 63

Apocalypse of the Heart 65

No Moment of Silence.. 67

No Voice of Oblivion 68

The Point Has Come... 70

The Indelible Moment 71

Aura.. 72

This Was Paul... 74

Once Again We Arrive at Oblivion 75

Lavish Yourself 76

Which Space and Time is Weaving...................................... 77

For Daisy 78

We Are 80

Twice 81

The World Anxiety Built 82

Decide 83

Portents of the Second Coming 84

Haiku Orgy 84

The Burden and the Jewel 85

I Have Come to Fill the World 86

Poem 87

23 Skidoo 88

How I Am Unmade 89

Bring Only Beauty 90

I See the Resemblances 91

The Anti-gravity Polar Bear 92

Isolated Dangerous and Invisible 93

Psychic 95

Her Story 96

The Wild Horses 98

O Perhaps Perhaps 99

The River Within Us 100

The Crystal Worlds 101

The Treasure House of the Infinite 102

Of Criminals Great and Tall 104

Beaten in the Afterlife 105

Someone Has Given You Life 106

The Oracle of the Familiar 108

The Saga of the Dark and the Light 109

A Sudden Shift in the Wind 112

Return of the Flowers 113

Without Regret 114

There Is a Door 116

Forgiveness Is a Forever Flame........................ 118

If All Could Know What Knowing Brings 119

Poem on My 75th Birthday 120

He Was Our Friend 122

The Burden and the Jewel 123

The Rock of All Brethren 124

This Is What You'll See of Me 126

The Hug of Immortality 128

Without a Sound 132

Perfect Insight 2020 133

What I Give to AI 135

From the Muck of a Swamp 136

Do You Ever 137

O To Be Big Enough 138

Hate No More 139

O Heedless Endless Eternal 140

78 RPM Birthday Poem 141

Time Stands Still 142

Chilled 143

From the Throat of the Earth 144

Invisible Singer 145

Entering Solace 146

World Without Heart 147

The Voice Of Horror 148

The Spiral 149

My People 150

Out Of The Peaceful Nurtured Gardern 153

I Am All These Things And More 154

Ode to A Universal Poet 155

My Secret Sacred World 157

Acknowledgments 160

Empathy Road

Dedicated to Alex Buck

"In the future of these States must arise poets immenser far, and make
great poems of death. The poems of life are great, but there must be the poems
of the purports of life, not only in itself, but beyond itself."
    ~ Walt Whitman, from Specimen Days

I

On Empathy Road those who have loved us rise
    from the flames of our hearts like blossoms of fire!
On Empathy Road solace reigns
    and we can truly call ourselves humanity for the first time.
On Empathy Road
    nature echoes its cries for equilibrium
    when our own voices echo a universal truth.
On Empathy Road
    compassion is the way of all government.
We follow Empathy Road
    as it leads us out to the stars.
We follow Empathy Road
    leading us back into our own hearts.

No longer chastise the poor for not having,
nor the hungry for dying but for the indolent masses of a rich culture,
no, do not chastise the believers in universal intelligence, nor those who have been
face to face with God and seen the vastness of that starry beating heart
within their own heart.

Allow the light of love to fill each of us as it has never been allowed before
and wake to a world made new, made fresh, made of love itself where love
has burned in oil and risen in black smoke from a million chimneys.

Allow your love to give and share so that we are a united species happy
in every single cell of our blind humanness.

Invoke peace as though it wasn't tainted by a thousand wars over ten thousand years,
and which argues that we must be at war because war is our nature. Then
we will rise from that pretext and begin anew, no longer relying on the disparate
ugliness within to shape our destiny out of vengeance, greed and killer rage.

No longer be the child who suckled at the Earth's breast and then ravaged
the same beautiful mother, making all women secondary in her image as
the great provider at the master's beck and call.

No more remain the slaves of need, and the urge to have more and more to feel alive,
        in our soul's fury and striving as we are nearing a precipice
and over the edge love is falling and returning itself to the grand realms which
                        sent it to us
                        as a gift.

I believe in the great heart of my species, that it will lay down every gun, that
it will stop generating tribunals out of confusion and hatred, and find
the center of all things turning within its own individuated hearts,
to find beauty in the simplest smile and surrender to life like children
    to their hours of play.

For the generation of complex rationalizations I pray simplicity
For the generation of addiction and sloth I pray dignity
For the generation of scientific absolutes I pray mystery
For the generation of poverty and base drives I pray torment's end
For the generation of killers and their protectors through Might I pray awakening
For the generation of manufacturers and brokers I pray that love is the coin of the realm.

Forsaken dreamers who have nowhere to turn I want there to be a hand to put
        in yours, and that this shall be the method
of our Government, rooted in empathy for us all; until there can be no suffering which is
        not looked after, and no agony which is not shared openly by us all
until it is healed and that cure is to be found only in one place, which is love.

If I have grown tired of my witness to this infernal landscape out of balance
where are my brothers and sisters by my side, no longer arguing the finer points
of human salvation, but doing it, living it, expressing it as the one supreme virtue?

If I have grown tired of my witness to this nightmare which should have been a fulfilled
        dream, where are the other golden souls whose lives shine like fireflies
        dancing upon a meadow composed only of their dream of endless love?

Dare I go on without being ridiculed, without pointing the disparaging finger back at
                    hatred
     and the denouncements of weak minds, tortured by all they fear while
accusing and opposing love as weakness, as addicts to the rush of rage
produced beneath their skin?

Do I send them love and let them free if they are to become the new wall separating
          humanity from its freedom? To anyone erecting walls I say
let the only walls be those of love behind which a child sleeps
                    warm from the freezing wind.

That is how I am feeling in these days of war, and crime, while the rich steal the world
from beneath our feet, and have made the very policies of chaos which assail us.

That those who make the laws make the poor to shoulder it
when there is only the one love to govern us
but it is a buried law, one buried in dullness and beneath the weight
of poisoned generations born from the embrace of the one law,
                    which is love.

II

What good to talk of death, I who always fear it, although I am in no wise
                    naive, or one who has never opened a book,
nor cast my own eyes upon the dying flesh to watch its light rise? I saw my own father's
death, as he lay there limp on his tranquil bed, and watched white tufts rise sporadic,
to a place above him. But that journey, no matter how bitter is the end, haunts us all
          as a question haunts an answer which we believe can never come,
in a universe composed of ice cold space and foreboding. Chemicals on the dim spheres
          turning in the nocturnal distance, dance for us in a song as concrete and finite
as life itself. Why mention this?

Out in the starlight gently gliding are a myriad of forms we cannot begin to know,
          not in the twilight mist of our thinking, with its roots sunk deep
in the loam of matter and matter's hard-boiled keepers, who'd give rise to reasons
why there is no afterlife. It is best that way, to preserve the status quo, to keep
the coffers constant filling, secure beyond morality, while the decent pray,
and the innocent wonder, and the religions dominate by making God into a man,
          so that flesh answers to flesh, and the blood of the son is wine at the altar.

Yes, let us be drunk at our altars, and strip down bare in the woods to dance,
for the earth in full flower, and yet with all her riches spilling onward
throughout time and endless epochs of living beasts, children starve
      because we cannot feed them of this bounty. Ask the corporations why
they put their patent stamps on crops you cannot regrow, unless through
seeds purchased from them? If you do not find this odd,
then as one of them,
      their patent stamp has penetrated beneath your brow, and also bubbles deeply
in your blood.

Here is the chaos of our assumptions and disagreements,
woven in the fabric of centuries for us to walk comfortably upon,
while lifetimes of suffering enshroud even the happiest day and the happiest hour.

Deep within the bones of those who urge us onward a change is coming.
It implies itself, it intimates itself toward a new spiritual vision not of the norm.
Included is life itself as well as the everlasting, included is the reaction to war
and the wisdom to know why, included is the return to balance and addressing
            every inequality.
            Race, sexual leaning, gender, duality,
all risen in one spirit giving their voice; the workers who are denied their future
and the callous bosses who own their day, no longer viable throughout
            all humanity.
We are at the moment in which democracy must finally be born,
and all labor leads to security and comfort, education and healing,
not for the prosperous alone. Not just man, as we are at the threshold of
      responsibility for planet Earth, and those small voices
hardly heard will soon be felt in every person's soul. Why question death?
When the leaf is gone does the caterpillar question why he ate it?
The universe is calling to us within our own spirit: Ask.
            It is the great reminder.
Death awaits no one's question, as the universe calls, echoing
            through death's door, hovering above the roof,
                  bursting with illumination, as though evolution
                        was the word of light made flesh
                        and that word is Life.

III

There is nothing more sad to me than the spiritually bankrupt man;
    the ones without hope are not among them,
the child burdened with incurable suffering is not among them,
the families scattered across millenia in famine and drought and flood
                are not among them,
the shops full of sweating men and women, the stores full of clerks,
without unions, within the parameters of great need, are not
        among them, the young black man hustling off to war, because
there is no other work is not among them, no.

The learned who have given up their dream of unity with others,
        who work to assail those whose rich lands must now be plundered
        for the richer nation and the dominant state,
The young man hustling off to war, not him but his generals in their knowledge
    of the strategies of hell on Earth, the pompous leaders whose two faced lives
are the tribunal of nations, the scientists gaming the methodology of complete control,
    and the liars who deny them, the pundits of the clouds of chaos forever yelling
and generating rage and tumult, these I want you to know and understand,
        are the spiritually bankrupt. The sadsack souls whose
mouths curl around carefully constructed lies to pry open the dark places
                within every listener, entering through the opened eyes of the watcher
        even though they are as asleep, entranced by the macabre dance
of the language of filth, debasement and triviality which fuses the world
                into its final knot.

For all of those whose hopes are dashed,
for you beloved, sweet beings whose lives are frustrated and even agonized,
generations from now, the light which is of the few will be among the many,
                the stars of the past will come to each person's heart like
        an infinite melody which vanquishes the poison of the spiritually bankrupt.
Do not believe them. Work toward that future which because you can see it ahead
    is in a very real sense, already here.
            If you are afraid today, bitter before a coming end,
        there is no end in sight. If your fear is for your children and their children
    after them, know that the liars will be laid to rest because they are the future's
                                fertile ground,
mixed into the manure of their blind and wicked speech and out of which blooms
        beyond their day of reckoning, a garden endless as the night sky,
teaming with those, who today, would be called masters, but who will in that future time,
                be the friend next door.

How often we dash the hope
of the promised land, and make of it instead an illusory place where angels dwell,
built upon the edicts of a clouded religion, which the rain nurtures within
                    the ignorant soul,
until that soul must raise its head beyond the clouds of unknowing, like a great blossom
                    of light which is the central light,
            the turning point within each starry countenance of man.
There is that day, and many more like it. Our journey has just begun, not ended, and
            we will see the still and wonderful landscapes of a thousand new worlds,
we'll look with our own eyes beyond the speed of light,
                    in ships made of light where once mere clay stood erect.
            We will dance in light-years and call the vast, empty reaches between stars
                    our home, where in beds like those we sleep in now,
            we will find our rest at the end of day, in a journey universal and sublime.

I will meet you beyond the misery of the flesh, out where the shining
soul has found its peaceful day, where the new body is a body luminous
and unsuffering, where the insensate wretches and spoilers of beautiful thought
cannot exist. I will greet you among the light beams falling from a rainbowed sun,
and you will recognize my smile, even though we have never met, because
you felt it in your soul. I will feel you in my soul, and the fairest love expressed
will make between us a nova of sublime desire now consummated without fear.

In your arms will come the true melting and blending of everyone and thing
                    with the fabric of our transmuted resonance.
Often I hear how without conflict the world will be a boring place,
but I say to you, you have hardly begun to know the structure of harmony's gate.
Beyond it there are ways of life unimaginable, and heaven need not be understood
as only an afterlife state, and that we must build it in the here and now.

IV

When we gather who will we not welcome?
Together: what does that mean?
We are one: what does that mean? I see you coming from a far off place,
not in miles but that distance created by thinking, and I am reluctant to hold out my arms.

I would not welcome you if you have consciously harmed others, but I must, I must
give way to love and honor its meaning. I must bow before the faith in the infinite
that will arise inside you, and one day unify us both. I will invite you into my circle,
but I am reluctant, and I will judge your actions if they celebrate greed and control,
but I will ask you still to join us in the hour of ultimate solidarity and ask of you
only that you love.

The world is a swirling tide of pain within its own soul, through the chain of flesh,
where no thinking holds, and the reins of want is by brute force, and the captured prey
    devoured in agony quite real, as the churning of forms devouring,
        cycles through eternal pain, in the jaws of death, in a universe divine.

        Yet even here is the law, in its state of animal majesty
hunting on the grassy plain where mankind first opened up animal eyes and saw
beyond the veil of life, into the depths of time, that a gift was given which even the beasts
could sense, as one grew near and placed his raging head beneath a human hand,
        for the affection given of a beloved friend.
We are not lions, ants or bees, we are the ones who will move on
born of this Earthly place: Will we seed the distant stars or die, we can ask
and ask we must, but the answer always comes back the same, the chance you take
        is not of luck, but love.

V

This is the time and place for war,
it is the flesh of violence and uncertainty; it is the dream of death
and death's finality, for longing of the dreamer as the dreamer perishes.
It is the place of carnage and its rotten aftermath, it is the palace of hatred and
                              hatred's warriors,
the helmeted armies of madness, and their digital reflections in a million
                      familiar mirrors.
This is the place of Armageddon and the bankers who will profit from it.
          From here blood flows in rivers,
on the shores I find the dance of the drunken thieves, lost in their dream of taking.
      They dance as if hung from a rope, the rope of no conscience,
the one suspended above a dark void where their souls dangle, no better nor less
than those who rob society on the street. What is it that they so joyously take
along the shores of the rivers of blood? It is our birthright.

To own what is ours, this humanity locked behind walls of oil and trade,
          they have murdered the true inventors of freedom, trivialized
their freeing machines, mocked the thinkers who have done the impossible,
and when met with protest, killed them. Our birthright is a time-bomb ticking
in a hot and furious wind, as a sweaty infant covered in a fever rash is dying, who
          should have been comforted by salvation's inventiveness.

Who watches this beside me dressed in black and feigning death's best friend?
      Mimicking a fictitious thirst for blood, is this our age's archetype? Pale
men in the dark who shun the light, who open wide horrendous mouths
                  to dine on us? There is no image
more appropriate to define the state of society, unless, perhaps, complacence.

      When the light within each breath not
only animates each being, but is the home of all future worlds blossoming
      in my imagination, now stagnant, defeated, awaiting a true trial by fire. I am
impatient for you to wake up, dreamer shaking violently and bleeding out of your
                  dream eyes.
      For what other tears would startle you awake when tears shed by
the myriad suffering seem to have no affect at all? I am impatient for you to
grab love's lifeline and pull us to safety, in the shadow of a spiritual grace,
tranquil in its forested light, dappled and majestic as a temple made
              of overarching trees and mountain streams,
in empathy's strong but gentle hands, in the stream of love where the rivers of blood
              can never flow.

VI

Do you think the earth's poles will shift
without first shifting the polarity of your own heart?
What is so hard to understand? That shifting the point of view of Selfishness
to Empathy, is the only shift of polarity we need. What if that is the real
Apocalypse, the true ending of one world and the beginning of another.
It is hard to imagine a condition of harmony generated by such a shift,
especially among those who say that without conflict how will I grow?

Not one of us has yet to envision a world which has thrown out that old pretext,
nor can we imagine what comes after. Is that not an explorer's ultimate paradise?
To not find a world, but to make a world anew in which new possibilities
                    are discovered?
What would it be like to have the whole world governed by compassion?
Where all machines of war and defense of nation, were instead turned to taking us
                    out to the stars?
Here in our own backyard is the answer: to become the stewards who have
mastered life, not conquered it. How are we different from the animals?
We are the ones who will take Earth consciousness into the galaxy, we
will find and embrace civilizations older than the drift of continents,
but would they embrace us in return, or hide from our violent ways?

A world of Empathy is not one of violence,
A world that such a simple idea describes, throws out the old world model
of dominance, mayhem and control, because it is stale, it has been tried
                    for thousands of years and failed. To those who say
                we need the bad to learn what it is to be good, I say
            how many more thousands of years of depravity, murder, greed,
        war, and selfishness, do we need in order
            to learn that final, simple lesson?

O the passage of time
has provided many wonderful things, but failed us completely in respect
of what and who we are. Never has a civilization built itself from the ground
up, upon the recognition that we are spirits and our bodies miraculous
            full of the power to heal ourselves and our relationships
                        to act because the Earth is in our hearts
                    to decide the future where life abounds
                    to see beyond time
                to contact loved ones gone into the light,
            who can talk to us if we but listen,
        when we learn the magic art of action through our hearts.

The multitude of the arrogant in denial,
their days are numbered, for a shift has come. Hear the signal in your throat,
hear the signal in your mind, the poles within you
are shifting, slipping, opening up, to show you that
you are no longer merely mortal, and as all spiritual systems
have ultimately prescribed, compassion is the state of evolution for us,
and not otherwise.

VII

To neither be seen nor heard in the ranges of the senses; not eyes and ears,
nor hand to touch,
and not unlike the moth in its chrysalis, to leave behind a shell of who I once was,
while I take to the wind with wings I did not know I'd have;
that is the hopeful speculation. Out of the sadness
of that departing sorrow, out of the heart beat
and breath departing, out of the stench of atrophy,
the last glint of the lively eye, the collapse
from which you will never again rise, comes
a shadow, a mist rising for which the normal sight,
which is not the whole of seeing, is not suited.
In the narrow spectrum of our loss,
only the pining of the flesh, the full flower now gone, its hint
tenuous, ungraspable, separate, and yet I sense
the inner light attainable
as a longing beyond that threshold
to touch again my lover's gentle hand.

In the dark hour, in despair and when ripped from love and the
familiar presence, the hollow space complete,
the unreturning, unrelenting absence, to the buried weight,
to a memory made of stone,
held as the breath is held, nevermore.
For none seem able, beyond the grief and shock,
to penetrate that quantum unknown,
to speak except in prayer to distant deity,
envisioning a god and his angels, yet always laid upon the cold slab of doubt,
where death has lain, removing us all from love's close knit family.

That is why I never pray to a distant god, nor saints, nor prophets from on high,
    but to my family and my friends who have proven their continued selves
        to me, and allied themselves to make my Earthly life divine.
Chant the praises of the vessel, surely,
    which is flesh and magic chemicalized, within this mortal being.
The original sin is to want to not know and remain in ignorance, while in
    spectrums beyond envisioning are glistening souls more alive than us.

VIII

Opinions fall like drops of blood onto the snow,
                like warnings from the eyes of a million creatures,
            upon the sad dawn I will awaken to their silence,
        upon a landscape littered with the remains of the extinct.

If I do not want such a world I know you do not want such a world,
                yet such a world is happening daily,
            invisible to the distracted eye
        where miserable hope holds out its hand in poverty,
and where a single cent outweighs the dream of all creation.

Am I to sing and chant of love within this day of mourning?
This angry day in which I drop to my knees in shame,
wondering what has become of my humanity's open heart?
We began in the heat of our youth to end such suffering
but the brokers of distraction offered us a technicolor dream
and many chose instead to feel only while watching the macabre dance
                of actors in repetition, and the digital death
            portrayed excitedly in games of power and war.
        We began in the coolness of an evening in which the hum of mowers
across the lawn brought smiles of satisfaction for our groomed achievement.
Then we grilled a steak, and then another, and then another to fill to fullness
        of contentment, and look around
    at the perfect death we share across our vast and populous proud land.

Who will be the first to escape this nightmare?
To fly from this depressing place, and leave body and soul anchored behind?
Who will be the first to back away from the swindle of the everyday
and feel his roots clinging to the dead earth in desperation and grief?

When the dark oppression of the newly extinct washes over us
who will snuggle up beneath its quilt, stultfied and hardened in our once soft lives?
The tides of warning have washed these shores many, many times,
while those who give it their heart's own voice
are trivialized in the game plan of high finance.
And I wonder why, why we have become such machines?
The toys of stealthy, silent lurking demons, who whisper in the soul's
                shadow, 'win, win, win,'
         they are the winners in their multitude,
      who do not ever want to hear these words.

My sorrow is for those who cannot mourn,
         for those who will not feel,
though voices rise in despair, and the countless ears will not hear them.

My sorrow is for those who feel secure and politely talk of the good life,
with lips made purple by French wine, and books on how to cook gourmet cuisine,
and gardens of exotic plants whose weeping leaves may long
for places on Earth so far away, that moonbeams cannot find them,
and on the windswept soiled roads, from town to town and stopped
by endless cross walks in the city, the trucks pull up to the loading dock
and empty an agony in boxes for Detroit. For the richest cities
the boxes come, and boxes shipped that travel far, by road, by rail, by sea and plane,
fueling the sky with man-made jets and passengers all asleep,
while on the ground a child looks up in awe, wondering at the abrading sound
      and churning smoke in the ocean of the night, and my desire is
that he will grow into a world where birds still fly,
      and not a sky devoid of everything but a noisy, glinting jet.

Should I again speak of love, O Love Infinite!
caring upon the fields of war, and in the suburban homes of happy families,
and among the students in their schools,
and among the hospice workers who know what caring means?
Should I again speak of love everlasting, of the soul's true form,
of the spirits who are waiting beyond the brink
        of this hardened clay? Nothing will move you
to believe it is your destiny, to end the endless suffering,
      to cease the endless war,
encrusted in your flesh, as each must take and take and take,
as though a desert emptied us,
      and anger rose up from love to conquer us forever.

IX

"O YOU MILLIONS, BE EMBRACED!"

Have I written yet for eternity?
Even my heart says no, they will forget,
they will not know. Those few may find
a note which lived inside my heart
and since turned to dust, and if I
have written for anyone, it is myself.
The reminder to take heart, to have a heart
full of the joy which a visionary life can bring.
And if its pages or whatever form turns
to dust it will do so gladly, having given
of itself gratis, at no cost to a single soul,
and only that its spark can join with
the spark of another and lay down
side by side like two lovers finding
the single moment in which self
must collapse to find the soul.

Yet they would tell me there cannot be
a soul in all things. They talk of angels
and their outspread wings, but know not
the wings of the stone, nor the flight
of the dreaming minds of all mankind.

I have seen what I have seen
and know that the rapture so sought
is naught but the splintering of the chrysalis
in which larval man now dwells, that he may
open his eyes for the first time as a new being,
one who does not ask for another to save him,
and finds that the path made of a barricade of stones
is tread by wingless angels who are the simple
children, who will move beyond what they have
long believed, into a state in which they will know.

No prophecy need unfold, no great countenance
from the realms of a sphere thought of as 'on high'
to descend to us, as if we are not already members
of that highest place, and the makers of servants
for the trust of owners of mankind. No prophecy
need be restated a thousand times to make me believe.
I will not believe, I will know. There are a few
who read not to read but to discover, a few who
discover to shatter what has been taught, drummed
home, for the slaves of ancient tales, those
who are poor in spirit, because they do not know.

This is my love poem for you.
"O you millions, be embraced!" By the very heart
of all that love can tell, by the longing of the sages
of every time and place. The one stream is ending
because it must, and it quickens, rushes onward
ever faster, so do not hold on to the shore,
because it will drag you under to drown.
Let go and travel to the farthest places
man has gone, rich in the wisdom carried
through immortal time, not to a savior on a throne
but into the depths of your own hearts.

There, a jewel turning in a greater market place
than any you have fashioned by the pillars of finance,
by any your skeptics reviewing the economic systems
of a million greedy men, by dint of the greatness of music
as yet unheard, by the hand and the eye and open mind
seeking the freedom of all beings, not just those of a single belief,
a jewel on a pedestal made of the teachings which open doors,
made of the sense to cherish life in every creature, a jewel
which every beloved teacher deified for glory,
has carved a single notch, a jewel turning
on a pedestal made for every man, woman, child,
and is of their flesh and blood.

When I look beyond the storied layers of your one book,
I find it striving to tell you to be at peace and find love.
I hear its voice rising within my own, to tell you
to sing of suffering and the way to give to all,
that which the wealthiest possess, that whatever
nightmare of subservience created under the aegis of control
be abandoned as this jewel now rises, rises like a blossom
in the spring of man's unfoldment.
Who crawls from the rubble beneath the war torn street?
Who moves mountains to build hotels?
Whose dynasty of eternal wealth gloats in private?
Whose shame passes for but a moment glimpsed in the mirror?
Who holds the reins of the human soul?

Joy over a thousand thousand millennia unfolds
if you would but see it! Joy to calm the tornado of
the heart of man! Joy to lift from one's hands
the end of all disease! Joy to quicken the only medicine
to cure poverty! Joy to give back to each child
the nurturing intelligence of love! Joy coming off
the torture rack! Joy lifting off the severing blade!
Joy encountering only joy!

Where you have failed joy rises.
Where you have fallen upon your prey in the darkness of hatred, joy now rises!
Where you have looked into the mirror and saw your own death, joy now rises!
Where you have turned upon another and taken what they earned, joy must rise!
Where you have lied to sully others, joy must now rise!
Where you have caused an agony and destroyed, joy must now rise!
Where you have been the brute, the smug undoer of another's work, joy must arise!
Where the liar has lied, where the snake has bit, where your handiwork
Was the turmoil for others, where you brought death and despair, and smiled
Upon the blood dripping from your own hands, joy must now rise!
Upon your words which denigrate and hate, hanging
Like corpses from the throat of these proclamations, joy will now rise!

Is this the bliss made of the darkest inferno of your own hearts
laid out as your final gift before the infinite? What salvo
from our depths; ugliness, depravity, despair, doubt, booming
in death from which sorrow becomes a radiance full of joy?
That and only that is the roadmap I would share.

Know this. That if you do not know, find out.
That you will find out. That you will have learned.
That out of your material gain in which
thought and deed has brought profound despair,
Joy will be the flower which lifts its ultimate head
and all futures will bathe in its fragrance.

Know this. That if you do not love. Learn love.
Unless love rolls from the wheels in your chest,
driving you through life, and know
that liberty comes only when all mankind is free.
The law which is love is not found in the convoluted protections of the rich.
The law which is love comes as a silent thread wending its way
up through the majesty of the human soul and heart.
The law which is love forgotten, drips from our labor.
The law which is love rests in the fists done with their beating.
The law which is love sits in protest and also swings down in the baton of rage.
The law which is love surrounds each bullet ever fired no matter the size.
The law which is love grows in the horrid tumors of every kind of cancer.
The law which is love must be recognized so that it may heal what is sick.

I have not written for eternity but to myself alone,
for I do not know who would listen or care.
I have no strength or courage to wrest from you your
sleep, your stupor, your momentary flash of all goodness.
I have no way of prying open whatever rigid thinking boxes in friend or foe.
I do not and cannot write the great writing
for I am not great until I love.

Offal Sings the Wheel

How the grist can love the mill which grinds it!
And when the mill is finished with
its grinding, dust to dust,
what is there to love? What is my soul
that of its wonders I make
powder for the mouths of babes?
Is that the argument? To be full
at yearning's end and never
to begin again, through lifetimes
lost to wander: not a memory wrought,
nor one fragment glimpsed; no
revelation of the power of those loves lost and won,
nor the skills built of my labor,
nor the wry laughter of the once-child's 'let's pretend?'

Is this philosophy's revenge?
To take us down again and again,
to arrange the suffering, knowing, and striving
into an absent grief? Who would take
such pain from me
and erase my very life beneath the churning wheel of time?

How much striving beneath the wheel
to make up-rising into gold? How much chaff
from straw to sew the bread on which
our timelessness is built?
Is it sweet oblivion that infills each enriched loaf of day?
Then lives that were and will be, to me, erase
the self, its lessons and its pride: gone
is memory, gone is fear of death. Gone
the night's glad music in the ebb of birth.
Nothing wrought into new bones, the ferment
of firmament to catch off-guard souls.
This is the rage and this is the calling,
but is it real? Is it the dawning
of unfettered awareness, or its dissolution
which we inadvertently applaud?

If Electricity Doesn't Crackle

18

if electricity
doesn't crackle from your voice
shut up
begin again

if the high mountain brook
your eyes full of blue sky
the living secret beneath
the icy rock
does not fly out
of each word
like a flock of quail
in a glade then
reach into your pocket
full of magic tricks
which a ten year old
would be proud of

show me your little doll
in a carriage full
of dream toys

i would love to hear
the music you play
inside your head
when i press my ear
to your cheek

Who Comes in That Hour of Darkness?

I am a worm in the Tequila of politics.
I am a spider in the wool of the sheep.
I am the hook which drags my species toward wakefulness.

I am the love of life inside every coward.
I am the phoenix inside the boiling egg of enlightenment.
I am the courier of the ancestors in spirit.

I am the thought which precedes action.
I am the calm center of all rage.
I am the empty space inside the box.

I am the artful face of the clown.
I am the healer of all agony.
I am the knife which cuts the anchor's chain.

I am the infant in your womb.
I am the wise man laughed at as a fool.
I am the unabashed delight of a playful child.

I am in the beginning and in the end.
I am the smile of forgiveness lost in anger's storm.
I am the open window you had closed.

I am the leaf blown by the currents of time.
I am the time to get up and get ready.
I am the wind which settles upon the still waters.

I am vanquished fear and love.
I am the thief who steals only sadness.
I am the eagle of the light of dawn.

I am a window into your own soul.
I am the electric spark igniting freedom.
I am the unmasked presence of the future.

I am who comes in that hour of darkness and terror.
I am the feared shadow inside the living shell.
I am who comes after the silence of oblivion.

Once in a Dream I Saw a Man

Once in a dream I saw a man
who was gifted beyond compare
No ordinary man but an angel walked
whose eyes held fast to the starry firmament
and whose wide heart embraced his opposite

Then one day his path descended
and his eyes looked down
and sadness gripped his soul
and the chill that passed for everyday
fell like numbers to the floor

Lift him up cried his friends
Lift him up cried Eternity
But the sad man looked for grief
in empty pockets where the last coin stood
and his torn life faded into ash

None could lift him and none
could set him on that olden path
for mired and wallowing in his selfish grief
the man with golden sight went blind
the man whose heart embraced it all
became the pit of sullen worry and concern

Such are the crushing blows he dealt himself
He exchanged his gifts for the price of pain
and a learned man in sad repose
looked for the glowing heart
now buried cold and dark

While the Chimes Which Mother Bought

The night is golden and the unpleasant dead
share shriveled skin beneath the rain drop eye

Towers happily where your eardrums played
among the cell phones dinging merrily
aside the vacant eyes and gossip marmalade

I'll try to divorce you tenderly
not an eggshell nor a flower break
where sponge blots blood among the tinsel trees
and our shameful heads throw sorrow to the floor
laid upon our feet like sexy painted nails

I held an agony so deep
your mind reeled and bowed its sullen weight
the hour of our love has ended
the snarling hounds lick the open gate

Cold has blown the air conditioned door
The exterminating hand may reach for cake

Outside the hired gardener leans
upon his rusty garden rake
and speaks a language only secrets know
where sex and shivers go to hide
side by side in the darkened hall

Now rigid hands numb softly crying
Jeers of naked guilt climax all wet
and weight unlifted licks the boneless flesh
while the chimes which mother bought
from the porch are gently tinging

January Third

Into the cold
breath of winter
she dissolved.

Into the night
and also
the following day.

Was she a snowflake
adrift from a sky
full of snow?

Was she a tear
among many droplets
of eternal
sadness?

Not a whisper
emerged
from her room.
Not a hint
of moving air.

Nothing which is
seen, felt, heard,
hated, loved, turned
its expressive face.

No. One snowflake
landed like all the others
and disappeared
among the millions.

One tear fell,
but not her own.

No word
was spoken.
Not her own
nor any other.

Her gift,
only for herself
was her own
silence.

The Root of the Flower of the Sky

plant a rose in adversity's eye
but be sure to poke it in there good
and hard! then sprinkle sunlight liberally
in the brooding conservative heart a-raging
for may it's stubborn stance melt like winter ice
beneath the warming sun
if
you can take the reflections of the dusky hills
which fall upside down upon the lake serene and still
where way off a loon warbles like a lonely heart
and tuck anger into its fiery bed with a mother's gentle hands
if
you can move the blackened stone off the tomb of a frown
if
you can uplift one cocooned heart to feel its butterfly take flight
so that it may go join the realm of butterflies
so that it may ride the song's windy blossoming
so that a care which was bound up and held in a dizzying web
can again fly off into the sweet pure day
you will know
that the root of the flower of the sky
is your own happy heart

Caterpillar and Snake

life and love walked hand in hand
through the town and on the sand
to the beach and into the sea
and into the hearts of you and me
(but we were busy eating candy
and laughing at the moon
because it hung there like a huge
blob of ice cream without a cone
and we were higher than the stars
on milky chocolate bars)

thus love is as love does
in our pants and hearts and minds
when our rascal eyes (those happy gardeners)
are raising flowers from our smiles
ah so sweet the thunder rustling between
our thighs
to cause moonbeams from your eyes to my eyes
to slink and slither like a caterpillar and a snake in love

when i touch you are the sparks stars
are the stars flickering birds into the dusky purple sky
and is the night folded kitten-like and purring in a quilt of light
where your hand rests upon the hills of my adoring smile?
my love for you is like a chariot of racing wind
a moonbeam racing a jet through the heart of the earth
a trapeze dancer flinging love between the strings of the night
an open jar an open book an open heart
ah love is walking lightly hand in hand with love

and the gray earth dances down the street
on happy playful feet
not caring in the least
what the crowds may think

The Task Which Must Be Mastered

Who is the spark and what is the fire?
The rich day, even the richest day,
Can it be a remedy? I see the losers brooding
While the cheering crowds sense relief.
Do they know how raw their hands will be,
How blood will run from their own sore fingers?
How will the completed task be revealed?
Like a tombstone or a shiny platinum record
Which we enjoyed? Whose mind suffers this,
And whose mind rejoices? Tomorrow awakens
Like it always does, over coffee or juice,
But can a man move a country? When will
We learn that we are more than the vote,
We are the task which must be mastered,
Not by others but by our own bare hands.

If Only

i mourn and always in the night i cry
for her fingers long like rivers moving
into every hill and moonlit valley of my life
now gone where i am ever seeking

i laugh and behind each laugh a minor agony arrives
like a train of coffins adrift through the night
of endless sorrows taken down to depths
too solemn for my mortal eyes to hold

my hand lets go and finds instead a greater weight ungraspable
that falls lifeless into the empty sky where hope
and sleep must blanket me but instead they strip me bare
and leave my aching heart to die exposed

what world is this to shower us in pain
and take that hand her own to cut out life
never becoming always and always as the dusk
to fall inside me like her secret death

In the Real Forever

I

It is an age reflected
in pyramids of cardboard
and cities of glass and steel
disintegrated in a flash.

One day
you will know only the fields
and your city;
then you will plumb the depths
of the seas and space. Allowed to,
only because you've discovered
that you must take with you
your little piece of air.

Breaking out of the confines
of all this 'structure,' this change,
we discover the indestructible self
reaching
throughout the depths
of Time,
as if Time were a veil, a
veil made impenetrable
by ignorance, and
because you cannot see
what is as real as a rock
but more invisible
than the air.

The Soul
has its eye on many lifetimes,
many dimensions. Deathless,
and always alive, we learn
that the story is continuous,
and that there isn't a today,
or yesterday, or tomorrow,

but that Time fans out
into a beautiful spectrum
in which there is only Now
and It is Infinite. There are only
hardships created by our smallness.
Fear is vanquished. Pain
is accepted or transcended.
Death is no more ordinary
than a door: and we are freed
to discover
the unobstructed regions of ourselves.
Here, insight becomes a window
one can look through,
or a door one can walk through,
"anytime."

II

The Present
becomes Timeless ---
and filled with variables. We are
creating the World
unwittingly. Our thoughts become
Reality, but the process
goes unrecognized,
except in flashes
of insight. Thought's power
is Creation. We
Think the World into Being, molding
into substance
whatever we desire. We think ourselves
into being what we are:
for we are the products
of our thoughts and desires.

We see only that
which we wish to see
and call it "the World."
The doors of our senses
lock

into physical dimension,
drawing all focus
into materiality: when
looking out to the stars
or "searching the soul"
we come upon
the True Expression of God.

III

We are unconscious gods
making a World, then not knowing
how colossal
our achievement is. We forfeit
responsibility for Creation,
for it appears as chaos
and hardly manageable.
But our inventions work
and our achievements possess
an aura of importance,
and the environment responds
to the directives of our minds.

Reality becomes a portal
opening in every direction,
and wherever we go
we continue to experience
in the same fullness,
with the same vitality
we feel right now.
Like Arjuna
upon his chariot
you may have to decide
whether you wish to die
limited by an idea of Oblivion
or lift aside the veil
of narrow thinking
and experience
whatever kind of reality
awaits your coming.

IV

It is expressed
in the Tao Te Ching.
It is explained
in the Vedic texts.
It is presented clearly
in the Bhagavad Gita.
It is drawn out
in ancient mysteries.
It is symbolized
in Egyptian Hieroglyphs.
It is demonstrated
through Healing Power.
It becomes a Realization
through the Tarot.
It is dramatized
in Shamanistic ceremony.
It is embroidered
as a Tangka.
It is encircled
as a Mandala.
It is unveiled
in Ritual Majick.
It is a message
coded into the Bible.
It is made manifest
by the Kabbalistic language.
It is wrought in stone
as the Great Pyramid at Gizeh.
It is the Huna
of Polynesia. It is
Stonehenge and Avebury
on ancient alignments.
It is the High Self
of the World.
It is witnessed
in Meditation.
It comes

in a Realization.
It is danced
in a thousand Yoga's.
It is an Alchemy
of Transformation
felt by everyone. It is
embodied as the Crucifixion.
It is the open door
through which we greet
the Soul. It is
our task as warriors
in a struggle. It is
the Breath of Infinite Being
awakening in our hearts.

My House and My Rock

i will not open my eyes unless to see your face
and become the drifting fingers upon the river of your nakedness
we suffer so that we may feel fully alive
destiny hurtles past grabbing us in the hope that we will follow
i dream that i am falling into you to become your flesh of love
i am a tendril wrapped around your ankle like a sandal strap
i place myself beneath your feet so that you may walk only upon my
Gemini air
i am the flock of tiny birds who dance in the sky to delight your sweet eyes

o how the tiny spring leaves dappled along the river bank are you in flower

there is no beauty but through you
where you once rested in the morning meadow red flowers now bloom
there is no greater miracle than to be loved inside you
you are the fire of my death and my springtime
your love is my house and my rock

Live in This Willowy Land

live in this willowy land
to hold upon my icy hand
here, here is what the insects gnaw
here is what is offered to the whore
what i offer she will ignore
it is only money i abhor
but is it money which i offer?
the rain has come
the rain has passed
the rain has drowned the insect path
now it's parched by noonday sun
the withered worm
is likened to the willow branch
as i spat upon the dry brown ground
through darkened glasses which i wear
to avoid the sun
to avoid the stares
to hide the hatred made of steel
which climbs through sinews
which we feel
about our distrusted fellows
and their skin
whichever skin they're draped within
as i turn my back and walk away
into the brightness of the day

Woman as Star

Who will lead us? She
is with child. In her art
a vision which pulls us, one
by mortal one, out of the womb
of her body, which bleeds
in the birth of herself.

Who will lead us out
into the next world, the one
born of her striving, to make
motherhood and self expression
rise, not like a moon at night,
but in the blazing fury of
a sun? The woman
who gives us endless
saviors from her womb,
the woman who, nestled
with a lover is the
celebration of desire.

So powerful, that a man
with bulging eyes trips
at her feet. Her power
is not what we give to her
gladly, but as a bow string
pulled ever tightly she
must spring beyond
herself and us, so
a generation not yet
born from her wet thighs,
will point to her star and
proclaim that the heavens
circle her, as the creator
of all beings and their ways.

The Rock which Holds Us

shed the stone-self holding us within
if we have become stone
split the stone
see what the heart will see
beating in us all

most have taken chisel
to the stone
carving the names of love
upon the surface of their hearts

but the deep blue sea within
no hammer
no blaze
can touch this

i look through to that day
the chilly sea within
turns depth to ice
and raging fire is
the icy rock of lives

then upon that season's floor
i carve my plea
help me o my lord
help me against
the terror of this dark
light a candle in the dark
where the party blooms
and neighbors come with festive food
to talk of sports and politics
drunk and laughing in the dark
that same dark cold
frozen on a shallow shore
where swimmers swim no more

beyond the stone that is the heart
beyond the mason's shaking hand
a glimmer across this frozen room
reveals the silent ocean deep within
frozen as a sheet so thin
a child with tapping fingers breaks it in

is there magic held within?
is there death and silence in its depths?
where is that laughing mob i hear
the stony faces on the path of djinns

come into this world
to practice death
to lie beneath that lair of ice
i found within the stone-made heart
where the murder of my flesh
becomes the zero of a future start

will i replace this frozen world
with one which empties into the sea
and make a solemn vow
to burn more brightly than
the heartless ghosts i see as man?

and who among these men so cold
even when they walk their walk
swagger on the streets made plush
i see their talk as naught but dust

that is sad
that is the sadness of my way
an error blindly leading me astray?
an error of their stony hearts?
and in my conscience bold
that ugly story must be told

so the one lone ray
which is my test
defines the all
within my breast

The Chess of Blood

The poet opened her mouth
and out fell a king. A king in love,
the romantic king she so wanted to marry.

And have his baby. Even if it was ugly.

But that was never her hope. Her hope
was a mirage of a bygone world, the one
we think we imagine, the one which didn't
have toilet paper, or medicine, the one
in which men bent beneath religion hunted
other men, and finding them tortured them to death.
No, not Iraq, and certainly not the Taliban,
she/he wanted knights laden in armor, who rode
white steeds through magical forests. Not the
forests full of zombies you see today, but forests
full of beautiful sylphs in flowing gowns and maidens
in love with princely men, who could not possibly
smell putrid, because in romance there can be
only sweetness and joy. Never checkmate
among the polite bishops with bloody hands,
and timely rooks with bloody chests.
Only rivers of wine, and chivalry protecting beauty
with the warmth of their blood caked swords.

If I Could Write the Breeze

If I could write the breeze on a summer afternoon
I would
If I could write the robust smell of a field where cows graze
If I could write the ozone and the lightning which proceeds from it
And the opaque roiling green of the most foreboding storm
And the awe as it mixes with terror as the blood pounds through
Our hearts and when the sudden silence as the storm lifts moves
Into a sigh of relief
I would
I would write of the kindnesses of decent people who act only with
regard
For others
I would write the trembling of the fingers of those whose desire
Presages the naked embrace and make their passion raw as rocks
Tumbled down a ravaging mountain river to the lakes below
And if lakes could not contain such a torrent I would write
The ocean as it swells and sinks beneath the rocky shoals

If I could write the rhythms heard when the big hammers
Slam the pylons deep into bedrock and the humor of men high up
On girders welding the steel of future cities
If I could write the stars over them freely scattered by the infinite
Then comes the solemn chore of making universes unfathomable in
Our small minds so that we grow and count like kids all that we cannot
even see

If I could write the enjoyment I feel for you whom I have never met
In a place I have never been except in my own mind
I would
The one who is full of caring for the animals and who thinks of them
As equals
The one who can tell the story of the grandfather's day of war
The one who laughs in rhyme and the other one who puts her mouth to
his
The sister of my poems who shut her eyes on this life
I would write them all into being

I would create them over and over
I would fill the world with such as these
And no others
As that should be the legacy which I write

If I could write so that each word blesses those who read them
If my words healed the loved ones ill near unto death
If my language was detailed enough sweet enough
To gather the grains of sand of our moods both good and bad
In the fertile day
In the embrace of love
In the hour of understanding
In the hand shake of forgiveness
In the repose of reflection
In the darkness before time
Where the first dazzling spark of love
Began to write us

Do Not Follow Me

follow the dots
and if they lead you to another's heart, you're lucky
follow the rain water trickling down the sidewalk to a penny
follow the scent from the diner like a magnet connected to your nose
follow the rainbow and its golden conclusion will bring you to the gift
of further mystery
but do not follow me

follow the banner held high in the parade
follow the track left of the meteor which rocketed overhead
follow the path of the ants from a hole to a feast and back again
follow with wonder all that is of the earth
but do not follow me

do not follow me into the darkness which is my darkness
do not follow me into the rawness of my fears
do not follow my anger crackling its chemical lightning in my eyes
do not follow where i would lead you
alone in the bitter cold and dark to a place inhospitable to humans
do not follow me to the precipice not to jump but where i must stand
alone
do not follow me

follow the lines of words which talk about war
follow the bullet invisible in the air until it strikes
follow the cry in the night until you can pinpoint its location
follow the rails and the rivers and the trails of jets through the sky
follow your hunches and your dreams
but do not follow me

follow the stories and lies as they unfold from your governments
follow the path which leads you out of your small box into a larger box
follow the sordid details about the celebrities and their infidelities
follow the end of one age into the beginning of another
but do not follow me

do not follow me because i do not know where i am going
do not follow me because my map was written in blood
do not follow me to the brink of my own self destruction
do not follow my truths nor my half truths nor my wild tales
do not follow me because i would only lead you to where you are right
now
do not follow me if you are looking for oblivion or emptiness
do not follow me

In the Bright Golden Chill of Morning

in the bright golden chill of morning i walk away
in the swift blaring traffic of mid afternoon i walk away
in vehement protest and threats of violence i turn and walk
i walk away i drift away

from the ugly face of political insistence i walk away
from the conniving liar and his smirking accomplice i turn and walk
from the all too stony face of the thug i turn away
from the mischief makers and their costly pranks i walk away
i turn and walk i drift away

alone upon the pavement of a desolate street i stop
surprised by new sounds coming from the trees
little whistles signal among the high branches
delicate little birds too shy to stand out boldly watch me
i move my hand and they flit away

i drift to them enchanted as i might to the whispers of a lover
they come from far off and they will leave in an instant
upon their music i long to fly and drift away

they sing their songs and drift in loping flight to other streets
leaving me upon the silent pavement where i stand
the ache in my heart and feet now drifts away
happy for the fleeting sudden gifts as they depart

The Ring and the Flesh

"How"
is such a small word
yet round like a ring
issuing from our lips
so full of
exclamation
and indescribable
fullness
so incapable
of preparing someone
for what is to follow

It cannot hold
what follows

cannot contain
the story
we might suffer

of
one of us
in a multitude

How this time
will roll out
like a wheel of horror
through its simple
three letters
the so-called reason
for a victory
of hate

How
like a scream held in the throat
not for a moment
not for a day or a week
not even a month
but for three years

Go ahead

Breathe
that many times
calculate
the stale air moving
in and out
of all those lungs
to fill a year
a decade
a lifetime

That is how
long the ring remained
upon her finger
the same length of time
it took for public denial
to come into vogue
for those whose ugly hearts
refuse the eternal shower
of love except
for love of
self interest

Not the ring
of marriage
not the ring

of graduation
not the ring
for anyone's happy engagement
but
a ring given

by a dying stranger
at that one moment
of her sickly
last breath

On a wooden plank
which was her bed
in a place in Poland
where the Jews
were kept

That ring
becomes
another's flesh
and will never
be taken off
not in this life
not in the next

The Empty Plaza

I have never seen an empty plaza,
there are always the pigeons
who gather to the guy with
his bag of crumbs.

Scatter the bird feed
and they will come,
they will come ravenous
and like locusts devour
whatever hits the ground.

And as soon as his bag is empty
they go
and do not return,
except to give a cursory glance
hoping for a remnant
of that recent feast.

Even a twitch of a muscle
can then alert the pigeons
whose eyes flick
like little shutters,
behind which an empty head
gawks awaiting
that one new morsel.

What if it never comes?

I have never seen a plaza
empty of pigeons
because always
someone arrives
in their loneliness,
in their hunger to be
an attraction, to fill
the emptiness inside,
just as he filled his paper bag

with crumbs
to gather the hungry birds
to his feet.

He sits in solitude among
the pecking and blinking
rats of the sky
who are driven to return
by his bag of crumbs,
like an audience
to whom he dedicates
a bag of crumbs.

A Beggar's Song

He sings of what he cannot see,
with songs that praise the beauty which
his eyes will never hold. He sings, he sings
because his soul is a map laid out by a God
he cannot know. He follows the road with his voice,
the road through the map which is his soul.

He sings because he hopes,
he sings because he must.

The beggar's song is a map at his feet
upon which he will dance, like a madman,
like a man whose passion is a river
overflowing its banks, a river made of love
which darkness can never touch, because
he cannot see the darkness which others see.
He only knows the blinding heart of love,
and sings, and sings, and disappears in song.

Those who watch and listen
may toss a coin. They may see
the many faces which are his,
in whatever country he has come.
They see themselves inside his song.
His blindness seems to help
their hearts along the road, the road
which is a map within his heart,
the map put there by a God
they cannot know.

The Red Woman

For Arina

She comes
and the wind upon her waves in blue flames

She is the graceful fire
burning away fear

She is the number which goes up
in the gambler's smoke
of the bet made red with his anger
of the bet he did not win

She awakens the blood to rise
from the ocean depths like a whale made of fire

She surfaces like a droplet of red from the wound
dabbed clear with a piece of tissue

She is moving in the flames which hypnotize
and which cannot be contained by seeing them

She is the liquid fire of the stars
She is the center for the spinning worlds of the heart

Her aroma is that of burning forests
The animals of the plains run from her encroaching flames
but I
I run toward her
arms outstretched to embrace her furious wind

The beating red wings of the approaching phoenix
as she emerges from the ashes of death

The raging storm within her steadfast gaze
Maker of worlds

She who renews the barren earth
The one who scorches red the green grass

Whose kisses drive their fire down through my red blood
in the fire of life itself
burning out the windows and tenements
of our night red cities
She is the flickering neon light cast up to the clouds
the red upon the sleeping eyelids from a nearby lightning strike

Her heartbeat of pure flame singes me awake
Her heat has taken my breath away
I am compelled to rush into her searing bosom
like the stupid moth addicted
to the red warmth of incinerating light

Flame is my mentor
My ecstasy
My best friend
My beloved whose sexual power roasts
other men alive whose
oven is red with the blood of delicious man-steaks
whose dark moody heat seduces women
whose flames of enticement moves governments
whose magical wiles precipitate cash out of the burning air
generating red fortunes for the gray men
asleep on the sidewalk below

She is the volcanic rush of lava
the rumble within the molten depths
which rises like rage to snare entire populations
and when calm makes new rock for the hardiest ferns
to squeeze in their new red roots in the slow tide of red life
as the blue world smiles from her lovely ruby lips

Out of the Emptiness Arising

For Paula Krier

Out of the emptiness arising
like a shawl over an arm to comfort us
like the green mist of the forest canopy at first light
like the mothers' smile upon the cradled baby
like the glint of love which absorbs you into a kittens' yellow eyes
like that laughter which comes up in the throat of the one you love
like the momentary greeting of two strangers in sudden agreement
like the full sense that you are healed and need not suffer
like the spark inside of you igniting an inferno of belonging
like that moment in which you are woven into the fabric of forever like
the stream of life felt pulsing within each breath
like a trillion doors flung open simultaneously inviting you within
like the moment in which who you were is now made of light
like the spirit like the ghost of dreams and longing like the fathers' hand
all inside you all caring for you all embracing you all which you now are

The First Stone

A woman of wood
can feel no pain, and
if desolation takes
her passion, there
is no room for
anyone's remorse.
She is wooden so
she can burn.

A woman of moods
and flesh and passion
is still a toy. Her man
is no mortal but
a spire who rises,
cut from the
mountainous rocks
of righteousness,
whose finger,
discharges
law and lightning,
made of his solid
pride, frail as
an infant's wound,
stolid as the pillar of
his house of sand.

These will not pass,
but stop upon the glory
of her sweetness. Those
whose wrath will cast
a bounty of ignorance,
knotted into cold rock
to knock her down
and open her, fresh
to the light of day,
like a pomegranate
splayed to reveal

its rosy inside
to the open air.
Her cries would sear
the breathy air
from the shouting lungs
of men, but will not move them
to forgiveness, nor commend
her innocence, which
can't be heard above
their predatory animal roar.

One finger lifted,
stops to feel itself
pressed to stone, stops
upon its heavy smoothness,
to feel how round,
voluptuous as a breast.

A finger full of spellbound
fantasy, full of secret
rendezvous and deceit,
to trace its shape,
made heavy with
his need to kill.
This first stone
which can never
stop its flight
will end her life.

Bring Only Beauty

Bring only beauty
to lay at the feet of despair.

Here is what I take from the dusk
to wash storms from your eyes;
the silences fertile with love,
moments drunk on the wine
grown in the fiery groves
of passion and surrender.
I have charmed the sunset
from the horizon to bathe
your sorrow. Deep
inside the living shadow
where you hide, I descend
and sing the songs which
death will follow
to lead him away from you.

That Strange and Seamless Sky

I do not willingly suffer your ideologies

Awake and alive I am yet asleep
Your nerves are my nerves and
They effervesce into the night
Like sparks from a fire built
In a circle of rocks in a realm of total freedom

As I stretch out these thoughts
I am surrounded by the stones of triviality

They try to contain my fire
To keep it only rising upward
In a single smokey column
Into the ever famished mouth
Of the infinite sky
To keep me looking only at the sparks
Diminishing in their silent ascent

Hoping
That like them
I too will disappear
Tiny fading unimportant in
That strange and seamless sky

Clinging

Grasping at the wind as it blows on passed,
can you hold it? How does it feel in your hands?
How does emptiness feel to your touch? That tightest grip,
is it you holding onto yourself? Pulling back into your loss,
all that is slipping off into the unknown? Protest in vain,
each will mourn as they do, and their solitary cries
can only be valued by another's naked heart:
This is how they mourn, this is the expression of their pain.
Hold them in your arms to see how solid they feel
and know their sobs as your own, as they are the same.

I Walk Among the Comets

i walk among the comets stretched as an old shadow
enjoying their exuberant light while i am etched in gray
which their eyes born only to brightness do not see

the withered and the frail reach out to me
their tired sad hands snap like brittle twigs which winter has drained of
sap
if i try to touch them

delicate the way icicles are delicate and which a warm youthful breath
can destroy

the glad comets bold of heart and playfulness who rejoice without even
knowing it
who celebrate because that is what life does moving through them as a
thread
of vibrant energy etching its light across the dark firmament

i walk among the comets dim and old and their twinkling eyes twinkle
for each other
sending messages of lust and fun and that pure love which inseminates
because that is what life does moving from one's genitals to another
like a spring between our legs creating life without horizon
i walk and the comets fly
i sink and the comets fly
into the deepest most beautiful blue of the evening
which for whatever reason my entire being hungers

to be filled by it as if to die i would become that darkest blue
and drape myself from end to end of the coming night sky
to embrace the flitting comet's light as children of my soul's loins

Dead Ode

For Richard

I am only alive because you are alive. I wash myself in the life and
death of others.
I paint myself bright red because I am bursting into metaphoric flames.
I brush the soot off my eyes so that it may float and make the air crispy.
You are love only because you have allowed love back into the hollow
of your chest
where your heart would beat it up, but instead kneads it into bread.

I come to where you are going, to watch you go.
I wave my dead arm to bring you back to life.
If you are going into the light you will have to cast a shadow
or at least carve a flame in the air. I will await your fire
with a pail of water. In it I will plant your fire
so that it may grow fierce and take over the world.
Only the fire of your love should rule our world,
and grow like fire weeds and water flames.

I am a swamp full of softly purring cat-tails. My eyes are two rivers
looking everywhere for you. While you are the rising and falling ocean
waves
remember to visit the beach where I stand calling your name.
Every now and then lick the toes, and fingers and hair
of the ones you love. Moisten our faces as you crash
against the rocks and rise up like a symphony full of snakes above us.
We will watch and smile as you have always made us smile.

Plain and Hollow

Plain
and hollow are
the faces
of men and women who pass

ghosts still in the flesh
skinny
lithe
able to play
tennis able to run
far
through the stagnant day
the idle day
the day of stiff hair all

except for the dead eyes
those dead straining eyes
that look as though they want to
rip from the face
rip away from the cheeks
which jail them

tear from the hollowed bones
sinewy jaw muscles
which have turned into steel plates

hollows
where plain eyes jump free from a face
and run
dragging out its soul in long strands

and I don't blame such a soul
its terror its
need for escape
because nothing
can live in there

in those plain and hollow sockets
without
fleeing in terror
from their numb web
from the unflinching cold
of the petty tyrant buried like a corpse
inside his own body

The Screaming and Screeching Sky of Her Ecstasy

The screaming sky the screeching sky
the ball bearing sky and beneath
a fuselage for the one I love

The tongue's incessant licking from dream to dream
where her hair is a dawn covered in fossils
and the murmuring brook of her voice
leaps with rainbow trout and the hoof print
of a gazelle one tired gazelle asleep on the bank

Those are my eyes that gazelle its black eyes
alert with wings and ready
to fly to carry the twin moons of her breasts
to the sea the gentle rolling sea
from dream to dream upon the isolated beach
and summer's tongue licking forever licking
its way into the screaming sky the screeching sky of her ecstasy

Whole City Limping

The whole city is limping.
It has gotten up from its place
rooted to mother earth and dragging
pipes, cables, sewers, and gas lines,
has gone limping off
on legs of splintered wood,
to moan about how much
it hurts to walk.

Summer
has crawled back into its iron-lung,
complaining how hard it is to breathe
in winter's frozen air.

The sky collapses down
naked to the earth
croaking to help her,
"I've fallen and I can't get up."
Nerves
gone numb,
who used to feel vital,
relaxed and delighted
in sensual pleasure,
now encapsulated
like vitamins gone stale
on a storeroom shelf.

The world is crippled,
a patient limping to
get groceries, on
legs now spindly
like a spider's legs,
the same fat spider
from last night's dream,
squashed beneath
a mystery foot
from so deep

within my psyche,
I will never know
to whom it belonged.

Legs
who limp off
into the dream,
gnarly like branches
buried in the snow,
unable to lift their
own weight, now ride
in wheel chairs,
made of charcoal.

Even
the stars,
so long suspended
on invisible ropes overhead,
hurtle to the ground,
busting open like bubbles
to dissolve in insignificant deaths,
where my once happy feet
are solemn gravestones.

Apocalypse of the Heart

These are who
We take through our lives
Hold them close
It has begun

The days of transformation overwhelm
We will suffer and we will hide
The walls are thin
And shake like children shivering
Hold them close
It has begun

What falls the tree
What takes a life
What kills and resurrects on high
Stay together and be steady in the storm
Hold each other close
It has begun

Robots fly
Like spiders up above
They see through walls
They see us all
Cower among your lovers
If you can
Hold them close
It has begun

Men without
A conscience ride
Their joysticks far away
To roam like death
From a window into time
Time will stop for some
Hold them close
It has begun

In a detached place
Which deals out pain
Mend their wounded hearts
Mend their broken minds
While weeping salted tears
And praying for their souls
Hold them close
It has begun

No Moment of Silence

For Richard LaValliere

Raise your voices! We are not the ones who loved the silence,
but the loud streams of noisy song and revelry.
Revelry may kill us even as it sets us free. I rejoice in who we are,
in the music which we love, in the loud laughter shared, in the private
moments lost in sound, in the deafening ring trailing afterwards even into
sleep, in the scratchy voices, in the lovely voices, in the shrieking voices
and dissonant chords, in the bad food, in the nights continuing into dawn,
in the parties, and vices, and desires met and unmet, in the wow of
watching lovers kiss, and drugs taken swiftly when no one looked, in the
drinks backstage or in the bar, in the endless sharing of music of every sort.
No moment of silence, but to raise a loud triumphant scream in the face of
death. Here we are you bastard, here are your bleary eyed sons and
daughters, you will cut down with your rakish scythe. Listen to us roar,
listen to us roar in a million decibels, so that the night explodes with our
voices. No moment of silence for any of us, but a blast of guitar, a wailing
voice unanimous, a fearless rage against the inevitable. No moment of
silence. No moment of silence!

No Voice of Oblivion

who is a mirror made of glass fearing its own fragility

celebrate the fragile within says the darkest shadow I am your friend
moreso than the man you hold between your thighs more than the
dearest lover

and the celebrant collapses drained
because she cannot evoke the stubborn light

no matter how willful and how much striving
the fret which is beneath glints its bloodied teeth
smirks benignly as if to say I am your lord and your test

I have to tell you that you can't move further until
the energized negative runs its course

in order to survive bathe fully in the living water of laughter
the trembling voice
the shot relationships
the friends so nearly inside you they are far far away
the parents and uncles of abuse
the men who exhausted fall like emptied husks along the path

but ah the path its strength and luminous eerie glow

beneath your heart's indelible foot print
moving like a dinosaur through the underbrush
stalking the beast of other adventures

I have to tell you that you are the
movement toward and away from
the victim and the victor in a single mutant instant
who thrives in a destiny both a cage from
which the caged bird sings
and a living fossil in a raiment of flickering shadows
also a cage
also a freedom

such as how the sunlight ignites the iris and
has a beautiful shine
so feminine so much an object of artfulness
seeing into itself

and the reality which is an uncontrolled
swirl of images growing immediate roots

no sooner does a thought arise then it
instantly roots itself
and once the storm has reached a fevered peak
the roots seek darkness as its drink of choice
lifting glass after glass to an emptying life

The Point Has Come

That point has come
when words rise silent
into the sky, attracted
like a magnet to emptiness
above, held there in
deepest blue thought
about the wonder there
and all beyond
in which a single breath
takes forever flight
exhaled once and only that once
allowed by the decree given to us all.

That point has come
in which we pass from self
to stand before the final dream
which fear has summoned,
as though upon a cliff we stand
motionless against the mystery
of the void and make our peace
with who and what we were.

That point has come
for the shadow which
was secreted within
to rise in wordless silence
a visage to itself alone
perhaps delivered
dimly from a final pain
of body grasping breath
and beat of heart
to a very different world, apart.

A few will glimpse
this passage in a glance
fraught with doubt
and lessons never learned

in all of days
and all of lives combined
even when an oracle
has made her point
and her oracular knowledge
is crushed like salt.

The Indelible Moment

The indelible moment has carried you,
O child cradled in its arms,
through years, as the one youthful moment
had swept you off your feet, and flung you
headlong into future happiness.

You have lived there inside a memory
and it has kept your dream
alive and constant. There is
the place you have lived, inside
the one joy, the moment made constant,
the flow turned into a whirlpool
of a thousand reflections,
all of them mirrors upon which
to paint the eternity of a self kept young.

Aura

You are these colors seen
in the corner of an eye
given meaning
having form
like cloaks of revealing luminescence

You are these colors interpreted
gestures of the soul itself
shining through normal light
telling a story in and of the moment
soul shine truth unuttered
running like a serial
enacted upon the indelible skin of the soul

You are a history in colorful array
a dazzling spectacle for the eyes of those dead
like a book of feelings printed upon energetic pages
turning in circles spaced out down your nakedness

This we are while we live
giants built of tornadoes within the flesh
seen front to back and deep within
showing where disease has rooted
as those same tender spoken words of love
as truth made bare was whispered

As deep fears and disenchantment lodged
deeply inside the curable wounds of ill-health
organs illuminated
the moments sliding into collision
the joyous times between friends
the deaths and births of every experience
shining a beam of light into the house of all incarnations

We move through the forest seen by eagles from above

The unwinged readers of souls
may come if invited
invite them
let them speak

We each are the same
a spark of that one cloth
in which all stories are origin woven
from our single faint thread

Make of us tiresome machines
make of us a labor depressed
a struggle which concludes
no matter the joy taken
no matter the sorrows endured
until that living aura contained within
surrounding us either dull or brightly
soars above the mountain tops
into a dazzling sky colored by all of us

A raiment levered from the bones of thought
wrenched from our secret lives upon the transmuting surfaces
of our future histories

We are shown standing naked before the infinite
from which nothing can be hid
a tattle-tale adventure reeling through time
in which we are predicted and warned
as though time was an uninvited doctor
holding a stethoscope to the pulse
of all that is happening

You tell your wordless tale
in moving pictures
the ancient sages infused their precise symbols
beyond our flesh and bones
to stamp our spirit's fabric with a universal tale

This Was Paul

I listened to his insights
and admired them.
Could I say the same for you?

The world is layered
in diversity. Some dwell
in anguish and pain.
Others live their distraction
because they must.

We studied first
the possibilities of
an afterlife. This idea
was fed by scientists
calling Consciousness
the core of all existence,
the bedrock of bedrock,
the shaper of steel and mortar.

We needed say nothing more
than that, while others need
embellishment.

To learn is all.
Learn to think.
To be is in process.
To be in harmony is demanded.
To unwind the choking vines
of trivialization mandated.
When you can love
yourself in your own eyes
a step into the day
is charmed. Toxic
people are allied
to destruction.
He tried to nurture
all such as friends
because he was a healer.

Once Again We Arrive at Oblivion

Once again we arrive at oblivion,
but I cannot believe it. Paint our going
with blackest colors. Add the screaming salt tears
of loss, the absence of a touch, being recedes
into past, the place from which we will not return.

Once again we arrive at oblivion
like the devoured animal whose taste
lingers upon the devourer's tongue.
We walk in the shadows of death
into the heart of its dominion, and wait
in our agony for its silence to speak.
The voice that will never return.
The vision of the final goodbye.
The pain and hopeless anger stops briefly.
If we are alone in the caverns of death
who speaks to us, who shows us their parting?
If I am a reasonable man how can this be?

Once again we arrive at oblivion
and its shadow parts. Go there
where the light is seen and friends await.
Where a world opens like birth itself,
to reveal a glimmer of its revelation.
To reach through the veil of death
from inside of death, to touch
our grieving hearts with a living fire
burning doubt into cinder and lifting us
into what love has made eternal.

Lavish Yourself

Lavish yourself in daily life
without scorn, without certainty,
where the road rolls
through the swirls of
meandering time,
like a musical note held in
its cup of echoes and
distances,
droning first low, then
higher, until it disappears,
lost in mist,
and wonder. We are that
wonder wandering,
sometimes
blindly, stupidly, remotely,
yet steadfast because
until we stop
to feel the isolated
thicket of speeding
reflection, the only
mirror which lives inside,
isn't made of glass, but is
seeing itself

Which Space and Time is Weaving

Life goes merrily on
singing its song with or without us.
It makes a paradise for itself between
the moments you are asleep or
waking. It covers us in darkness and
sudden luminescence from within the
very heart of the earth.

Beneath our feet and bounding
through the sky it soars invisible.
A harbor within its tireless wings
is keeping an eternal, watchful eye.

A flight of joy through rock and softened life
it touches whether born or unborn.
We are the living stuff of its flight
uttered before and after the depths

 which space and time is weaving.

For Daisy

The oracle who was my Teacher

My friend, can I call you such?
You are like the canopy of stars,
my blanket, the comfort of
happy faces when you are happy,
the wind-swept summer sun
for the playing children. Can
I call you these?

You were like a mother,
a great bird descended from another realm,
a tree to withstand any storm,
and you came
to me for me,
and to us
for us.

A mystery wrapped in wisdom,
a birthday gift wrapped in poetry,
a magical language from a magical world
not my own. In your world
angels weren't angels but artists, dancers, dreamers,
and poets wrought their poems in gold
to lay at the feet, not of gods, but of ordinary children.

They surrounded you with their playful whimsy
and saw that you remained one of them,
teaching them also, how
to always remain as children
in a stiffly contrived world
conspiring against our dreams.

You made us the allies of rebellion,
quietly moving against
the tyranny of the mediocre.

Can I call you teacher? My learned elder? A lover
who cloaked her affairs in mystery, yet offered their beauty
and eventual despair in the only worthwhile language of the heart?
Your struggle was our struggle, your students, your friends,
who embraced fame,
and the limelight and who
shaped the culture of modern times
secreting your name beneath their words,
your influence, your delight, your muse,
without which we would have remained
buried stones the world keeps dark.

We Are

We are amazing beings
each unfolding a story
upon our rounded surface.
From deep within we see our story
built from an edifice of thought.

Bones wrapped in sinew, the contraction
and expansions of life throbbing
and aglow. We are made of magic,
so they say, and it is true. Our
numbered days, for many fraught
with pain and anguish, plod on
until we can't. Some blessed with wealth
beyond measure, others as starry eyed dreamers,
and more who just think and whose work
is taking us to the stars. Each a separate story
full of mystery, tragedy, love, laughter,
a vision, a truth, a lie, a fabrication,
a mortal reality transfiguring all the rest.

Twice

I am lost
in the ozone
of my own storm.

Searching?
For what? Life?

I already found it
because it was given to me
twice.

Just as death
was given to me
multiple times,
so that I might see it
and understand
what spoke through
its mouth.

Just like a minor Hermes
I delivered its messages
determined to be
accurate, precise,
unerring.

Death taught me
to be unerring,
decisive, but life
taught me otherwise.

Life and its storms
cloud my path.
Until like thunder
itself I shake upon
the firm ground
without its doubt.

The World Anxiety Built

Brick by brick anxiety
built a shell. A dark prison
with a mail slot for a window.
From the distance
a cold stone castle loomed,
medieval carved granite
which had been flesh.

Inside the food queen played,
until relaxed she settled outside
in her wicker nest. Smoke curling away
in a self made breeze.

How to love someone
who makes you feel uncomfortable?
Whose brick cell you want
to tear down until its stone
shards burst into bouquets
of flowerless petals?

The floor now echos
with the dull thud of a cane's
bleak rhythm. The isolation protects
what shouldn't be seen. Pain
controls self-worth, turns it's face
toward death.

Whatever happened to happiness,
carefree? Now like a garden
full of dead butterflies, they lie there pale,
lost color sucked into the earth.
And everywhere a loud ringing,
composed of ticking revved up
to the speed of light.

Decide

set aside the trembling
thought
about to shake itself to
bits
the clamor of little
troubles
which assail each of us and
inch us
toward a false oblivion

we are either opaque
against the sky
blotted out and
insignificant
like a thousand year old
match
buried in its own charred
wound
and not its flame once
brightening
the flame of unlit others
whose
need to burn laid dormant
in the unrealized deep
dark

decide which to prefer

to burn brightly for a time
or not at all

a choice to go through life
a torment
whose joy remains unborn

while a jewel to which
paradise
has brought its flickering
ray

awaits the flash of
timelessness
within the moment
you decide

Portents of the Second Coming

as I fell I noticed a smiling face in the mud
as I soared I watched the birds turn into a woman in a blue starry cloak
as I ran the sweat on my arm-hairs wrote out His Name
as I looked at Joe Camel I saw male genitals
as I stared at Charlie Manson I saw a fallen angel
as I listened to the night the wind said "Holy"
as I turned to face a stranger I knew it was Don Juan Matus
as I searched the World Wide Web I found a new religion
as I read through Fortean Times I found God's face in a Nebula
as I was absorbed in MandleAcid fractals I met God directly
and we are now pals with similar interests

Haiku Orgy

I am standing nude
Fatter than i used to be
No orgy for me

The Burden and the Jewel

Do not deny the tiger's smile
even if you think he's just not hungry.
He sees every move you make,
and your stark stillness as well.

If I look deeply at
the eyes of a woman I know
I see such sadness
as can only come
from deep mourning.
It shifts and I see longing,
I blink and see finality.

The tiger sees a meal,
the woman sees her own heart
and contemplates that final moment,
cut short when it will happen.

Both have their eyes upon
the inevitable. One sees it as
delicious, the other sees
her body emptying
of all that is loved.

I carry a different burden.
Mine is the burden of
a life to come.

When flesh departs,
and a new form
shapes itself from
a hidden jewel . . .

buried as though life,
not space, was buried,
luminous and thriving
inside every atom of
that final change.

I Have Come to Fill the World

I have come to fill the world
with my dreams. To meet
my fellow dreamers
with their blossoming ideas.
The very architecture
of the future.

We wont need your oil,
your wooden education,
your cities of glass
and steel nightmares. We are
now on the fringes
of the possible, making
a world in which
a man can give
as much to the Earth
as a tree.

Poem

What does the butterfly say?
What does the new bud
opening to greet the
morning sun?

What does the quiet
cloud think of your
struggle to find a
truth?

Is the cloud
showing you
its freedom to
sail across the sky
surrendered to the wind,
happy to be a cloud?

There is proof
in every rock, leaf,
glint of an eye,
fragrance of
the perfume of day.

Life is stamped
by the proof of
death, and death comes
in whispers and
the tribunal of
an agony of surrender.

Like a
cupped hand returning us to
what we really are,
when it is done,
our eyes open, our
thoughts ignite among the
crowds who await

and they see us
being born to their
world.

23 Skidoo

i cry with them who cannot cry
i die with them who cannot die
i fly with them who cannot fly

there are those without mouths to bellow
there are those without limbs to walk
there are those without any sorrow
there are those who wont ever want to talk

i will paddle down the river of tears
i will scream into canyons echoing beyond sound
i will see into depths which render others blind

i am not alone and i am not a shadow
if i find a source it is because it was sought
if i am alive it is beyond the life of our knowing
i will not conceive with a false imagination

i will be pushed from my life and fly without wings
i will close my eyes and see without sight
i will join with those friends who tell me "Be Fearless"
when breath must stop and infinity invites . . . . i will not fight

How I Am Unmade

This cup, this room,
that very hand. Do
those things around me
make me who I am?

I am not free
except by imagination
alone. The physical,
once limber as a gazelle
now a burdensome weight,
made heavier by pain.

The bathroom scale,
the weight it shows,
is that me? How could
I weigh so much?
A private number, one
to fret about, to push me
toward weightlessness, perhaps.
I will get there.
I will return there.

For itself, like
a magnetic mist is
pulling me, intangibly,
increment by increment,
until breathless, I will arrive.

Bring Only Beauty

Bring only beauty
to lay at the feet of despair.
Here is what I take from the dusk
to wash storms from your eyes;
the silences fertile with love,
moments drunk on the wine
grown in the fiery groves
of passion and surrender.
I have charmed the sunset
from the horizon to bathe
your sorrow. Deep
inside the living shadow
where you hide, I descend
and sing the songs which
death will follow
to lead him away from you.

I See the Resemblances

i see the resemblances and start
not with a sound but a cause
and in the make-shift vehicle which expresses me best
i slip on my most comfortable slacks and shirt

wonder if it is a day for shoes or sandals and walk
heavy on my heels to the windows where i stare
down at the street and begin

i always begin in a never ending onslaught against stopping
then i recall the deep jungle aborigines of Indonesia and how

i don't want to be there because i hate the biting insects
and will never get excited about eating grubs from bark

and the blood-red eyes of those who hunt and eat men who cross them
are ominous like heavy tornado clouds who might kill

even those
they imagine may have crossed them
and i want to stay home and watch tv because
it is not only safe but entertaining

there is nothing wrong with this picture
to idle away your life watching stuff
and then talking about what you watch
and watching for what others watch
in the wonderful array of things we watch
when we are too weary to act
and love the doldrums

only i wish to interrupt these doldrums
for some hot sex
now back to the tree people of Indonesia
because they are far away and more real
then people next door

The Anti-gravity Polar Bear

The anti-gravity polar bear dances off the icy water
not realizing his furry flesh is gone Now he will hunt
in the negative the amorphous shapes of animals
without bodies whose howls grunts and screams echo
in the hollow of near space He will paw at emptiness
the way humans paw at commodities His breath rises
like vapor off a gas pipe in the now teeming realm
of all death If he was a visionary he'd sprout bat-wings
and soar forever off the mortal trap now melted away
beneath his proud once bloody claws

Isolated Dangerous and Invisible

Sometimes the dead
think they're alive
so they come back
to haunt us. Taking
vicarious pleasure
from what we do.

I see sucker fish
attach themselves
to sharks and get carried
throughout the sea
while the predator
makes choices
who will live
and who will die
in its wicked mouth.

But the haunted ghost
can't eat or drink or
even breathe, but
it can take because
the essence of that taking
needs no learning
it just is.

Next I come across
children wearing costumes,
at first they're having fun
but after a duration
perhaps of years
it becomes addiction
and they can never stop
dressing up in new costumes
playing as will any child
well into becoming an adult.
The ghost knows them
as allies, as who to seek

as a free meal to fill
up an appetite which wont quit.

And life goes on that way
day and night in plain sight
protected by the airy feeling
of fun, the very joy of wanting
and getting, under a very
special, magical blanket
which we never bother
to look for, because
we are taught that
our reality has places
to hide, and be exposed
by microscope, by telescope,
by electronic detection,
in a universe which
remains beyond sight and touch,
isolated, dangerous and invisible.

Psychic

Be merciful to those
who do not see beyond
the shadows of physical existence.

Be kind in the darkest hours
of your bitterness to those
who do not read between the lines.

Try your heart at forgiveness
when besieged by your own anger
within. Take deep breaths
of the light, and remain steadfast
when assailed by ignorant questions.

Spout platitudes as though
your life depended on them.

Sometimes you will fail
but over all your very energy
will bear fruit in all who dream.

Eventually the one source
will take each of us in and
destroy our separation, some
by degrees, others in an instant.

Each of us will stand naked
in our own light, and it will be
a signature of how far
we've come.

Her Story

I

A light descending to the Earth, her heart raises its own light in
greeting.
She is our beginning, of all things she is the key.
She reaches out with all her affection and we join.
Their coupling is the thunder and the lightning in the black sky.
She rains upon us and their light rises.
Like pages in a calendar of the infinite
Her loving hands comb time into braids and light years.
Whether or not we pay attention it is her dawn.
The child she bears now in her womb renews us.
This child who thinks and feels and lives outside itself
Is itself the first quantum singer to echo a billion centuries.

II

I feel her words, her ideas
Penetrate, digging into me.
Feelings automatically invoked.

No matter how I fight to remain
Autonomous and not feel
The pain from mere stories

My body gives in and the tears
Roll from my eyes, and that fiction
Overwhelms that drowning
Part of myself so deeply touched
Until like space itself
I breathe in new worlds.

III

Why am I not crying over the whole world?
How depraved my fellow humankind
Can act? The constant dying which needs
No reporting to come from the unseen
To negate happiness. The tortured people
Somewhere enduring agony at another's hands?

It's opposite, the real blessing of good souls
secure without want. Those who make wise decisions
naturally. Why am I not weeping, smiling, embracing
them? Moved by good action and signaled from
Soul to soul, in the mystery of connection
I cannot deny. She has brought us unity.
Her stories are a oneness unimaginable.

Arise from the fertile ground of her being
Like flowering plants to blanket us in hope
As though I was the earth itself like an infant bird
Mouth open in hunger gulping vastness riddled in words.
I spread open my own soul to embrace
All her stories, the vast, the minuscule,
The horrific, separating as an agony.

The secret of stories exists
In our likeness, which touches her beginning
Feeling her resonance, captured in her empathic depths
To weave the infinite into our majestic human web.

The Wild Horses

That moment when their hooves leave the thunder in the
ground, and for a moment, manes flying, the mustangs move
silently through the air like lyrics which must jump from my lips
or be forever lost

They would range where cities are now built and the sky itself
crossed by the ghosts of messages, streams in a tumult of voices
ever growing above the arid hills, a glossolalia built into a
tower of Babel, a flood inundating the pure blue invisible round
blanket over the world

Deep in their night they graze on the grass of human souls,
purring softly, murmurs of a time between human conquest and
human absence, alone, unkempt, and free

O Perhaps Perhaps

O perhaps perhaps
wonderful perhaps
perhaps i will not light a cigarette
nor take a shower for one week
perhaps i will one day walk on water but perhaps
i will already be dead
perhaps there is no life when i am dead
and the atheists are right
and all the scenes from other planes i witness are perhaps
lovely hallucinations
emblazoned upon the retina of my perhaps imagination

o you little smiling eyed child what mischief

are you preparing in that single playful glint
i see are
you in love with me? as i perhaps
have learned from you to play with freely lovely life
and have a seat on the wet wet grass
where the worms dangle out their tongues
now
smack them down into their holes!

make them hide from the giant's hand
perhaps they'll sneak out from behind
and sneer and get the ants to dance
uh oh that sinister reflection
that if behind the words in front
a makeshift play on thoughts derived
from fear of love and social bunk
perhaps you'll win my evil friend
and leave for me
a sickly world   (of feelings pale)

ack! perhaps i'll go and drink an ale!
and never look you in the face again
but stare to where the ants are free
to lick the sugar beneath my knee

with a charming child who teaches me
just what and what not to be
perhaps perhaps o wonderful perhaps
the child within will look at you and wince

The River Within Us

Place your finger in the icy rushing water,
how fast, how cold, the crystal cut which glides and joins beyond
during this warm day looking within at the perfect rocks seen in its
torrent,
as they expand and contract beneath the currents swiftly going.

Place your finger in the wind to dry
making a compass of your skin so you will know its direction
as it glides passed and does not need to join again as it is always joined.
I place both my hands to gather fingers full of your beautiful brown
hair
and feel the gaze of your two beautiful eyes as a warmth indelible,
magical, filling me with awe for you in the form of you, in the heat of
you.

In each such exquisite moment we share only here and within the
folded embrace
of each others' love, as it moves on, divided for a second and rejoined
beyond.

To feel the well of beauty within you rising to greet me, falling away
only to return,
again, and warm, an invitation inside your mystery and where your
thoughtful love
surrounds me, keeps me within your wet and perfect darkness swiftly
going.
This is more than you, than us, this blended healing,
this is the home and the heart of the home for all of us.

The Crystal Worlds

I have planted my feet
firmly in the here and now,
yet they yearn to take flight.
To see the wonders that exist
in many worlds.

As a teen I drew landscapes
in which giant crystal clusters stood
upon a silent plane. It spoke
of loneliness and beauty,
of the slow outward push
of atoms to shape a world
of transparency and angles.

Looking back it reminds me
of how slow evolution is
in the making of a world.
I added animals composed
solely of imagination, some
rejoiced, others copulated.
Some looked down, captured
in their forever pose, deeply
contemplative of the matter
upon which they stood.

In my imaginal world I
was the adventurer, never
knowing quite what would rise
from the subliminal within,
barely visible by my waking mind,
until like sleep itself, I opened
my inner eyes to gaze upon
the fantastical.

The Treasure House of the Infinite

We follow the trends
obeying the patterns,
no thought about it
outside of pure enjoyment.

Yet there is a seed beneath
held like a prize within the unknown
turning on a pedestal within a window,
slowly, like a diamond glistening
so we can see the facets
mirroring light and searching eyes,
not as a crafted crystal really,
because it isn't hewn,
and is made of us.

Awaken one or even a fragment
to anoint your tongue with its
nourishing charge, an elixir,
a drug of purest being, of light
and symbol vibrating so fast
like a golden spider in an orb
which you can see vanish
into its own speed while
still knowing it is there
nearby, if you'd but look.

We are like that, needing
to close what has occupied
our minds to focus elsewhere.
To look at the ground where
deaths are buried, like seeds
which can never germinate again
in our known world.

One of a multitude may guess
an answer and bring a hand
to touch what isn't seen as real.

To touch is to know and so
within every single breath exhaled
is our own death buried invisible
in the air before our nose and mouth.
The ticking clocks all vanish,
every single one, and what has
come for us to take us each, in
its hands as its own jewel,
to be placed, O lovingly,
into the treasure house of the infinite.

Of Criminals Great and Tall

of criminals great and tall
and all the sweet dead pretty birds
lying at their feet
the ones who stoked their fire
and the ones who stoked their meat
to make life pleasant for
the thugs they each desired
and clamoured up to lavish on

for what's a thug without
his worship and what is worship
without a shiny throne
to lay before and lick their crowns
with barren tongues and fires all aglow
from fevered brows and thickly uttered growls
which mean the world to all
whose hollow ground bursts
like bloody wounds into
pools for fools? ah, snakes

that learned to walk like men
among the hens and eggs
of barnyards rife with brawn
and sweet reminders of what money
is and isn't
and what power was
and always is inside their dream
of furies won and furies which
will win as slaves to laud the old
and make it ever new
so joy and death can be as one

Beaten in the Afterlife

I was told
that after
the Lodge
drums and warriors
stopped singing.

What came in their silence
was not an echo
but the sounds
of the Spirit drums
beaten in the afterlife.

Someone Has Given You Life

someone has given you life
cherish it
someone has carried you
in their arms
from birth
from illness
from a car wreck
from death's portal
cherish it
when you look up
into the eyes of love
cherish it
when a gift
lifts you
from poverty
in tired arms
cherish it
when poverty itself
turns away to say goodbye
cherish it

when those who hate
send their malice flying
cherish it
when you are alone
and loved
even from afar
cherish it

in all the days
of agony and tears
in all the misery
and ignorance
and toil
in all the gluttony
and merciless
men who'd

have you cower
and use you
to their advantage
until they themselves
must face
the tribunal of
their souls

cherish it
cherish it all
and give of it
make it your own
and set it free
for it has wings
and eyes
and a heart
as big as time
and in its
embrace
you are whole

The Oracle of the Familiar

They speak school but their lips do not move.
They speak a new language as it's created.

Shorthand of the old upon the tips of tongues and fingers.
Accelerating, always accelerating into the incomprehensible
Future. These ramifications ought to stagger

Yet they just pleasure, unfreezing what was static.

Learning which vaporizes
Words on screens vanishing
The sky

All nature doesn't welcome you. You may come
And you may vanish as it moves in a tide through endless depth.

Can you visualize, think outside
The small flat box which you hold so near your heart?
The purple one flowing along the white wires,
Its sounds disappearing inside
Your ears. The lavender one
Entertains your soul. The silver
One stealing the hours, is a labyrinth
Of games, yet
You haven't noticed. The minus and plus
Of all our days composing a new mind.

The oracle of the familiar
In which we fly through sleep
Toward a virtual dawn
Which was once just drifting sand.

The Saga of the Dark and the Light

Darkness is not the other side of light
Darkness is a small running boy and a small running Toyota
It is dark inside and outside
Light inhabits darkness
as it pours down upon a beach
full of sunny people

Sunny means cheerful not bright
If death is dark
Life is darker
Light hides wherever it wants
to be freed like suns inside bombs

When I move my hand darkness
swims around it like water around a fish
In my sleeping face the dream
shines through brightening the room
enough to read by

The tiny black insect is not absent of light
and isn't made of darkness

A blind man can see
through his tongue
whether it is light or dark
tasting hereness and the never of seeing
He sees the road as a snake of imagination
even when his eyes will never see road or snake
The darkness in his eyes is a light to all possible sound
His feelings are sight in perpetual dark

A rectangular cement wall is
the dark dam for a reservoir
as it fills with glinting rainbows and sparks
which magic can never hold

In an antiquated darkened tenement
Spirits see us as dark intruders to their bright homes

Light hides inside darkness like a jet hides in its hanger
Darkness clings to light like a lover begging forgiveness
Light is regal pompous stubborn adamant

When darkness feels unrequited the lights go out
People think the first moment was dark sparking an explosion
But it was a squeaky hinge on a door of forgetful firmament

Light opened its door and out flew darkness
like a slave escaping into freedom

We come from the dark and return to the dark
Dark is light is dark
The darkness of dark is the light of lights
I close my eyes to the bright sun
I close my eyes to bright sleep
I darkly dream the darkest light of darkness and only lightly

Lightly go the darkly darkenings
which lightning strikes

Rebellions come and go like dark tides of light
One dictator fades to black and another fades to light
My darkest thoughts are your lightest feelings
I rise into the light and darkness falls through the light
Nothing is faster than darkness
To travel at the speed of dark
Is to be at the end of the universe before it began

Out of the darkest womb of night I came as a newborn laser beam
A straight bright crimson line which only darkness can bend
Darkness is the Uri Geller of interdimensional travel
I like light
I like the way light licks my face when it is feeling its puppy love
I like the way it crawls into the dark of my nights with its fingers
And wakes my manful days into a sunflower of light

I like the way darkness crumbles off a cookie when I am not very
hungry

Darkness is the past and light is the future
but remember that darkness is way ahead of us
taking a snooze at the end of time
When we arrive it is already bright daylight
for the darkness has gone traveling through the light years

A Sudden Shift in the Wind

Every now and then
I need a little chaos
like a sprinkle of cayenne
right up my nose

It is nature's way
of moving me to
new insight, a broadening
of my view so that
I am not stuck
like a splinter
in a rock

Thank you nature
you are a good friend
I will wash myself in you daily
and scrub you deep into
each of my bones

They are creaking and
gnarly so every blessed
new thought germinates
as a friend who is
like a vine
climbing vigorously
behind my old hazy eyes

Return of the Flowers

Lost jazz and the plain
music of the leaves

Sweet summery fragrances
of a world in love

I touch your electric hand
and it pulses directly to my heart

There is a vision
in the seed and in the clouds

I am the house
you have placed inside

I live in the dream
you have allowed to be born

Our garden sings out
in drifts made wet in the rain

Without Regret

To greet that poet whose wisdom
is a ray piercing the sky like a laser.

And I am exactly what I have become
no more nor less than all my attempts
having risen to what flame?

A spark perhaps of that same light,
a mere glimmer igniting a hand
and its shadow flickering.

When you raise two finite eyes,
mere specks within specks
of that dazzling countenance
extending on,

like a stubborn contemplation stuck
in a shallow pit of self, and all the winged equations
of the masters of science and meticulous thought

flying into the invisible
on wings made of alloys of pure light,
going where you can only dream.

That day comes when the doorway
of chance quietly invites entrance.

Hushed and secret beyond any language
and thought which preceded.
Touched as if all atoms gave way
and the open world beyond
succored you, like an old friend
whose patience like light itself
simply awaited you to arrive,
shorn of suitcase and all obstruction.

Then in a blink all the world aglow,
extending outward and also inside
as a million friends whose greeting
is a radiant warmth erasing all doubt
with its welcome.

There to know in that single spark
which doesn't die away,
that we are that same stuff
which came before the stars and
touches each of us with its joyous hands,
empty of time, regret, mortality and fear.

There Is a Door

There is a door
which will appear
when no one
walks the road
with you

Alone ahead
you will see that
special door which
opens and then closes
only once

Your hand
will open it
and when through
your hand will close it
behind you

then it fades
and disappears

but love
which always lingers
at that door
will bathe you
in its tantalizing light
you will see
with eyes
you did not know
you had
and there around you
other doors appear
countless
opening and closing
by others hands

as far as you can see

and in that place
which can never
grow crowded
you will find
their love
which just
like yours
has journeyed here
and fades into
your newmade flesh

Forgiveness Is a Forever Flame

Wholeness may one day come or not.
But it shall beckon from afar, like a calling
voice in a raging storm, which deafness may deny.

The flowering shrub which springs anew,
a garden unto itself, thinking, ah I am
complete, and the fruit of all my labors
are this richness I presume to be.

But the hollows do not speak, they learn
and listen to the saga as it unfolds.
Making hollow judgments for a hollow
time on earth.

Yet forgiveness is a forever flame
glowing dimly under brush, a root
from which the groundwork speaks
to say it is itself the source
of nurtured self and winged thought.

Some will move and others stay
fixed upon the dung of time,
to make an angered sorrow swell
where in the depth of deepest space
there is not an uttered word where
silence, cold and knowing will prevail.

If All Could Know What Knowing Brings

For Leah

If all could know what knowing brings
there'd be peace in every heart,
the wars to win would wander blind,
and man whose unsure feet have climbed
will rise to heights on hardy winds,
and know of worlds and realms
where earth-bound souls
do not compete.

We are more by far
than clay-bound blood provides
and all our lives as living proof
will roll a map across the night of stars
which we will touch with living love
and tell in silence, light and dark,
of imagination's worthy praise
from mountain heights
and oceanic depths of soulful plight.

Rejoice right now in who you are,
rejoice in daily life and gain,
rejoice in what the dream night folds
an everlasting journey which has a name.

Beyond the artful names we gave
to newborn babes shaped from our love,
to aged souls in health or pain
who bear the burden of their lives.
We are each the light that shines within
to make a world which love must reign.
While worlds will rise from deep within
to spin their tales of sorrow, love and sin.

Poem on My 75th Birthday

I will alight upon a moonbeam branch
made of life and blossomed soul
to sing of joy and walk
through my open heart
into a sea of love.

I will turn from this broken form
and begin anew to make
a day of dream and a day of thanks
in celebration of
both the perfect and the fault
from which it sprung forever intertwined.

I will come to pass from this reflection
of who I was to who I am to who I will be
and not link one iota of remorse
to this river of the self
moving sometimes swiftly
and at times in shallow pools
where tadpoles play.

I will rise through water into flame
and rise from flame
into blackest emptiness
and know this as my home
where worlds become
imbued with life and death
in the cycles of eternal night.

I will fall and fail and drown and die
and in so doing know the frailty
of its vast sea of despair and love
to forgive what separates us from
those we've known and love forever
that we stop and start.

O grateful realm which turns us
into life and takes us to a distant shore
through the portal of the soul
while doubt pervades and visages
of the dead abound.

I raise my hand and cup and say to life
you have been fair
even when I was a fool
and treated others like an ass
and all that pain and woes
my ignorance has caused
will move through time
and learn of joy complete.

He Was Our Friend

a buddy and i once watched one of his roommates leave the room
by picking up his pet cat by its tail

my friend reacted by throwing him out of the house on the spot
threatening him in a most intimidating way
and unless he got in his truck immediately and drove away
for good
leaving his cat there with us

he did it saying
he never liked the cat much any way

we all liked the cat
and the cat really liked all of us

no one ever pulled that cat's tail
for the rest of his life
he was our friend
and we liked the way that tail
was always high in the air
with a nice hooked end
on it

The Burden and the Jewel

Do not deny the tiger's smile
even if you think he's just not hungry.
He sees every move you make,
and your stark stillness as well.

If I look deeply at
the eyes of a woman I know
I see such sadness
as can only come
from deep mourning.
It shifts and I see longing,
I blink and see finality.

The tiger sees a meal,
the woman sees her own heart
and contemplates that final moment,
cut short when it will happen.

Both have their eyes upon
the inevitable. One sees it as
delicious, the other sees
her body emptying
of all that is loved.

I carry a different burden.
Mine is the burden of
a life to come.

When flesh departs,
and a new form
shapes itself from
a hidden jewel . . .
buried as though life,
not space, was buried,
luminous and thriving
inside every atom of
that final change.

The Rock of All Brethren

This ocean of silence is us.
This deafening ovation
of spontaneous applause
is us.

This tiny blue dot
in an endless sea of death
is us.

The card deck of dimensions,
layered infinite tumbling ideas
is us. All behavior, all endeavor,
all fear, grace, destruction, resurrection,
age, youth, mistakes, corrections
is us.

Each turn of the world,
every moment of love,
each life lived and remembered,
each of the forgotten,
everything still unknown
the tantalizing dust of galaxies
the thought, the act, the sense,
the longing, living pulse and duration
is us.

Unity is us.
Separation is us.

Every predation,
every meal, every word spoken,
every hushed secret unspoken,
every single atom of the infinite,
is us.

And yet we still must learn to love,
we still must rise from our own hate,
our lives and passions which shine
with wise choice, with failed hope,
with misgivings, with separation,
with correction, with resistance to change,
with coercion and deceit,
with
war and death, and in that moment
we embrace all,
to meet the enemy with love,
until in a sea of forgiveness,
we are finally
the rock of all brethren,
forever.

This Is What You'll See of Me

This is what you'll see of me,
a wholeness, limp, inanimate.

What you won't see is who
has gotten out and floated off
nearby. I will make my way
on a new path, one not visible
and which wades through
your sorrow like a winged bit
of firmament kicking up
pony glad dust on golden hoofs
in a storm of sadness as I depart.

I will explore the visions of bygone worlds
and join the serpentine parade
of reptilian ages and flying birds
with wings thirty feet across.

I will rise to the tops of crystal mountains
and view vistas of civilizations gone and to come.
Thatched townships of wooden cabins
where farmers churn their butter
and daughters in long dresses gather
up their gardens made of light.

I will watch layered histories unfold
to rise like pyramids in festive jungle cities
one on top of others, and hear the pulsing blood
of their times as they rose toward ours, and past.
I will watch the brave explorers seeking
a new land in wagons drawn by horse and oxen.

I will descend into that glowing red world
built of sadness, rage and ignorance.
I may move there as a ghost and slam
their doors, and move the relics they think
are real but which weigh less than dust.

I will watch them climb to current times
to fill themselves on the thoughts of others
and hammer out their deadly game
in flesh of shadow and poisoned greed.

I will watch the giant auroch sway and stamp
in herds where stealthy hunters move like ants
with bows and sharpened sticks
in a sacred dance of life in fields aflower
with the ghosts of daisies and pink clover.
I will feel into other lives and other times
of primordial lands in which I once lived.
You will stare down at what remains
and say, "Is this all?" and I will not answer
having drifted into other worlds and futures.

The Hug of Immortality

I will go
and sorrow will follow.

My dreams say it all,
time is short.
Be complete.

Love life enough
to shift from suffering,
and despair, grieving
and remorse,
let people be themselves,
faulty and confounded,
happy, angry, sad, alive,
allowing them to stumble
and be tongue-tied,
foolishly not getting it.
Let them in.

I will pass
and time will erase
the sorrow which
they will feel.

Why do I
mourn the moments
yet to come? The probable
hugs never again to feel.

The embrace of a lover, passionate,
mouth to mouth, firmly pressed
together, two become as one.

Age has opened up my eyes
while others come,
holding bouquets of grief.

Into a rectangular hole
I will toss my own
flowers of farewell,
a sacrifice
of my own mourning.

Who I was
will pass. Mortality
strikes no bargain.
Fear or no fear,
the child of fact,
the aged old man within,
his thoughts
of dissolution, watching
life unending enfolded in
his most golden heart.

No dark shadow looming
to cause terror
but that moment
which each of us must feel,
the final draining of life as it
is born to a world
made of imagination and
our being once held within.

Who I am

is going.

No more the wise words
of resolution instead of revolution.
No more who I am,
here where my desperation
seeks others
just to talk.

My talk
has quieted.
My days blur as pages

I have turned.
My friends turn to
their own lives and
I mourn their parting
as I pass, as I go
my way.

My mourning
for myself
is my mourning
for everyone I will miss.
It carries a question
of selfish love,
for their tears
their caring, their
continued lives,
and happiness.
With no stonework
to visit, no distant grave
in a cemetery
none can find.
You will wonder
if I continue.
You will not
have learned
the art of knowing.
You will not see
where all of us
have gone. Few
will return to
show you they exist.

Yet I want to be
one of them who returns
so you can see and know
what I have seen.

I will learn that art.
I will find that way

which others found,
to come back to you,
if you but ask.

To visit for a moment
brief and profound,
which may shake you
to your core,

or be that moment
in which affection
and joy greets you
as your friend.

I will show you
that mortality
can open wide
and out of the silence
and rift of death
finality again will
place its hugging arms
around you
soul to naked soul.

Without a Sound

Split into pieces?
I divide myself.
Part of me wants
freedom and even
divorce from others
seeking the shadows
inside in which hiding
has its forests and isolation.

In complete darkness
I feel around
for others, finding
a face or two
which by touch alone
I hardly recognize.
They speak a language
alien to me. To me
it is like listening
to confusion
which to them
is clear insight.

I hunt blindly,
touch as seeking,
not finding.

Until I find
a silent place
and finally speak
to the one
who makes sense.

Without words
and also without
a single sound
it speaks
the plainest truth.

Perfect Insight 2020

for Shawn Stugard

       i have traveled
to
the border
and saw the

desolate

in the halls
where democracy
set itself in motion
but now where
the churning gears
of fate spawns
tribunals

i see men
so diseased
the world
is squirming
in their windstorm
of monumental death

i have peered into
the sick wards
and watched
the elders
dying

infants who would
cry if they could
but who wade
in dreams
of summer shores
and await
their
healing
if that were so

i walk our streets
and breathe into
my mask

and praise
each whose caring
hides its breath
shyly returning
air to air

i sleep and wake
alone at night
and wonder
for my friends
along this path
who clearly see
their truth
for it is just
and must prevail

What I Give to AI

We give the machine wings
I bequeath her my mind
see what you can do with my misspellings and ceaseless musings
I pour into her all of the raw palette of my poesy
Hate or love me I bequeath you my ambivalence

I feed you all that I have ever eaten that you may know my taste
if it comes out of you in a series of zeroes and ones so be it
I challenge the rawness in you made of bytes
to rise to the occasion and make it live and breathe

Of our mistakes as a species I just dump it into your beckoning craw
all that is kind and beautiful all that is astonishing and majestic
that I lay down before you upon a carpet woven of my destiny
that you may contemplate the act
that you may know we see you as a God
and it is a lie

From the Muck of a Swamp

Sometimes the most outlandish
picture begs surrealism. Please, surrealism,
accept my dumb image as graciously
as you would a world not composed
of genetics, but iambic pentameter,
replete with rhymes.

There inside a casing as thick as a cocoon
one day will emerge a butterfly, with huge
wings, belonging to an age in which the world
was steaming and the thunder is not from the sky
but the stomping dinosaurs.

Know this, even the delicate moth
will turn into stone. Crack the seam in the rock
to reveal the miracle, butterfly or moth,
delight and awe for such a find.
Will what I have composed excite as much,
live eternally like a stone, fashioned by
the handiwork of time and the muck of a swamp?

Do You Ever

Do you ever weep for all the suffering?
Do you ask, why bother? Does a tree weep for all the other millions
sawed down? The tree doesn't
weep for those gone, while it listens to the singing of the toothy blade
taking its own life. There is a
dissonance of the cutting blades with their teeth ripping through wood,
which makes the tree
wonder where its going next. To become a house, you say, a board?
Perhaps for winter warmth
upon the hearth in a man's house, the cozy fireplace from which its
embers turn to ash and the
shovel scraping through it makes a tinny yet full sound in an orchestra
as big as a city, only heard by
trees. Trees are not sages, and aren't silent as they yawn and hum like
the creaking boats swayed by
a tide. There is that, and that the shining stars are listening. Why cry for
all the suffering, you might
ask? It is how we mourn.

O To Be Big Enough

i look for you in mist and turmoil
i look for you in my pain and anger
for you i seek in the myriad abysses
my screams bare themselves of all clothing
they strip themselves naked until there is only bone
i listen all of my days to the faint echoes from a tiny voice
through lens and sound i scour the night stars for a vision of you

and there in the midst of all depravity
in the flooding grimace of winning vileness
in the unceasing torment of murdering war

in the folly of the jackals of the soul's poverty
in the deluge falling skyward in the vanity of brokers
in the wind fall of those who live free of the rest of us
i find you standing with rock hard obedience in the service of greed
for you living in the wounded distance i offer my full healing
embrace
as a prayer
as determination
as longing watered in hopelessness
to shower your life of horrendous despair caused by warriors of all
countries
and like a tall stranger bending to tell a child that its love is all that
counts
make for you a tabernacle of my opulence and the very
substance of my soul

there in the endless storms of grief
rapid-fired from human hate
i reach a hand of solace but it is too late
i cannot drag you from the ruins which are taking you from us
i cannot convince the powerful to stop your suffering
nor the most powerful from reversing time
in your lands of starvation and days of war
in the grief of your families and friends
the shape of what could have been but will never be
in the numbness of class difference and causes of dominance
in the pain caused by inattention and clinging
o to be big enough to set you free

Hate No More

You
do not forget.
The story must unfold
to live inside you.
To become a lasting flame,
one to cherish,
a human tale,
to teach others
what to feel.

Arrogance
must never win,
must never again
be allowed
its triumph
inside
the many
burning skins
of those who
lived to suffer
in the hands
of tyranny.

One day
they will all
have gone,
replaced
by other stories
just as wrong.
Until we
are strong
enough
in the thorns
of misery,
to say for
the rest of time,
from deep within,
hate no more.

O Heedless Endless Eternal

Of my outrage
at our history of war

for every drop of blood
for every death
in an ocean
rising red

our sinewed time
upon this Earth
its forever shattering
history
to make anew
the false and sallow ground
upon which each
agony must fall

what an evil fertilizer
from which the flowers sprout

and springtime songs
the carefree birds trala
from mate to mate
upon the sprigs and stems
of our human bones

My outrage
trembles at the thought
that we have chosen this

our lot

made from the bloody dawn
of our legacy as naught

forever drugged
by a war addiction
inside the wounded soul of man

78 RPM Birthday Poem

speed is
not as important as
stillness

illusory
nature at
its finest
making us

believe that
sitting in the silence
the stillness
the primordial
safety of a meditative
state is real

when in fact
we are hurtling
at 18.5 miles a second
67,000 mph
through
weightless eternity

the joke's
on us

real does
what it does
as we watch
the slow clouds
move like fluffy
dancers
in the
soft blue
of a
sunny day

Time Stands Still

and in it little figures move
play out tiny dramas in tiny lives
a woven weave that dances life
We come and part and then return
and suffer fools we love to blame
while the seething clock of time
stands sentry at the gates of paradise
O that joyous black which trembles full
beyond the break of day and endless black of night
made luminous beyond our narrow sight
where mystery dances upon all graves
and life itself in endless history
stretches out to fill that void
so still it would appear
an empty place when it is not
This silent womb will bear the weight of all that is
full of beginnings becoming and ends
in which eager man must strive to find his flaws
and fix himself to dignity or die
that and only that
is the message of the spheres
that we will conquer fear with joy
and make a paradise of our present lives

Chilled

i will be free of you and will not care
in the book of shadows everywhere
the stale perfume of a bygone year
has smothered love and broken fear

the yellowed leaf is not the tree
it falls and drops and isn't free
the hand of time has crushed its skin
the hand of wind has worn it thin

the icy wind might freeze my heart
the tranquil mood might break apart
the sheet of ice which is no more
has opened yet another door

From The Throat of The Earth

Harbinger of the deep
Cast up from the resounding depths
To fuel our sorrow and
To plunder shores

Reap from us
The birds and fish
O shining hand of death
Smother the shoreline in gleaming umber
Reek of gone ages
From the bowels of the costly pit

Urgent messenger
Broom of the sweeping dead
Come at last to rise
Like a cry of slime
From the throat
Of the Earth
To cover us

An Invisible Singer

It is not the singing
of a great voice
inside a theater
nor the casual man
on the street who
raises a plain voice
from his heart.

It is not the singing
of the frogs in heat
in the nearby pond

raised in a cacophony of sex
filling the night air
until they grate against
the listeners' hearing.

It is not the singer
in the pop limelight
enthralling an audience
nor the repetition
of those songs learned by
rote and sung to
oneself alone
or in crowds.

It is not the singer
blind and with a
guitar whose blue song
is as old and enchanting
as the muddy hills.

It is all of them
joining voices with
the invisible singer
who rises in the night wind
moves across the valley
rustling trees and
whose artfulness moves
the water and clouds
and the stars themselves

Entering Solace

The flowering mind opens its night petals
to bring in waves of dream.
During the day it is hidden among
the ticking events of every hour.

We are always learning and leaning
into other minds. They share entire dreams
in a storm of imagery, thoughts that come
like great cargo ships which evaporate upon
your brow and enter the darkly illumined places
within you, so you will know what they know.

World Without Heart

The shocking news
is that you do not listen,
that your wake-up call
comes up from your own darkness.
To repair this now
means that it will come too late.
As if we do not wake up until
everything inside us that was ugly,
mean, murderous, ignorant and afraid
has poured out, has maimed,
has added to the grief, and
worse, is killing us
in this instant.
You'd rather patch
the damages, self-perpetuated,
and never heed
what the inner-voice has said,
over and over.
As if
love was the last resort,
respect for self, for life,
for others' ways is out of the question,
until it murders someone you love,
deletes
something
you cared for,
takes away forever
your chance, everyone, and everything's chance to
at last be free. To repair
is to be dead. To not listen
is to be dead. To not know
that we must love
is to kill the heart's capacity
for joy.
And this, all this I see
around me, growing inside of me,
forced onto me and my children,
is the coward's way.

The Voice of Horror

I look at you as a fire breathing dragon
I look at you as an ageless desert looks at a spider
I look at you as a howitzer in wartime
I look at you as a downy feather floats gently in the air
I look at you meaning no harm
I look at you meaning all harm
I look at you from beyond the army of ruthlessness
I look at you through whatever mood I am in

I am ancient and I look at you as I would see children playing
I am ancient and I see you as the dust you are made of
I am ancient and I see into your distractions and horniness
I am a windbag a dead wolf a rusted snare a dead hunter
I am the cesspool you have at the end of all your pipes
I am those who drowned those who burned those you forgot
I am a number you never sought
I am a lie you told yourself to feel important

I am not a god but I am energy you have never named
I am before the beginning and after the end
I am who you will become and who you came from
I have opened my legs wide and birthed the myriad creatures
I am the erect pillar of male rage spewing lava into continents
I am the dead crust of the earth its mantle and its spinning core

I was born in the fire of suns and matter made of flame
I was the child you cradled in your arms
I was the tears you shed when I died
I am that dead thing who rattles the doors to all your cages

The Spiral

Dry, so dry
you
do not believe the earth pulsates and it is called life
here
right here where I stand
upon a trampoline net, a web of vibration lifting us
in a coil
through space

My roof
the neural fibers woven together like the fingers
of a child
a dwelling place beneath in which love
may circle hand in hand with death
and life as well
compose its neighborhoods and fertile places
streaming with the complexities
of the human condition

My religion

the autumn leaf rejoined
by others in their dance in air
to come to rest so gently on the silent walkway
The hum of transcendence in a droplet of water,
of the transmissions through cables of our daily talk,
joy falling into sadness, rising back into joy,
life which lifts, beating down transient complaint

Dry, so dry
you in your own hands
guarded in your approach
always wanting proof

while the real magic
ephemeral, walks through the corner of your eye
hears in near silent whispering
what cannot be believed

unless this world is spinning....not just through space
but a tale which pulls down questions
as if they were the stars

My People

I want them to live
more alive than they were
in their own lives

I want them to live
outside my memory
and inside my heart

I want them unbroken by life
but shaped by their struggles
finding each other anew
breathing the air
breathing in spirit

I will find them
rejoicing after death
in a world of imaginings
into being made anew

I will join them
alive in a circle dancing
in celebration and abandon
toasting the end of all wars
the beginning of time
now beyond embodied life
as family as friends as lovers
I want them to live in bliss
with me, through me

without old stale rules
the outline of soured lives
lacking joy or in the
stench of the dim
and dismal ordinary

I want them to live
in the extraordinary
in the frenzy and fun
of endless amusement

I want them to live
free of their struggles

free of the poverty
which sent them fleeing
from a world made dead
by authoritarian murder

I want them to rise
from the hay wagon
being stabbed in suspicion
by pitchfork and terror
by ticking time's
searching bony fingers

I want them made brilliant
mad poets artists philosophers
crazy haired scientists
with chalk on their noses
scribbling the designs
of numbered galaxies
the invisible motion
of immortality

I want them to acknowledge
the wonder of the infinite size
of a billion billion billion galaxies
as they might a cottage
on a country road

I want them to be free
like bird song
like uncontrolled laughter
like playing children
like students plumbing the depths
of their hearts and minds

I want them to come with me
into mystery into indelible memories
into the shape of all things past
into a future giving voice
to the present

into the impossible
into the improbable
into the unreasonable
into the dreams of children
into the vision of surrealists

into the body warmth of saints
into each other

I want them to be free
to be filled with light and dark
to be with one another
as the closest of friends
to take from all whom
they will ever know
and be that fulfillment
once invisible

Out Of The Peaceful Nurtured Garden

If you do not hear
the world screaming,
drowning in its own tears,
you must be listening
to your quiet garden,
happy to be nurtured
and loved so that it
can reach for the sun.

My dreams may not
have anything to do
with the suffering
of others, with their wars,
and the tribunals
which caused them.
In fact I find it stupid.
How on Earth (literally)
did we arrive at this
conclusion? That bitter
struggle is the only way
to express differences?

If I stand alone,
resolute that this
is wrong, that this
is a pathology,
it is because if
I was a sun, my light
might reach out
through space
and burn such
a world to cinders.

Yet rage grows
more rage. Even
when all of its
desire wants
nothing more
than the quiet
of a peaceful,
nurtured garden.

I Am All These Things And More

I am
all these things and more

The softness of a purring kitten
beneath a hand
the smiling child whose sweetness steals our love
that place within which quiets us
when hammer and anvil are at war
dark which is only a vessel for light
and light now invisible in the hallowed dark
the sting of whiskey's passage from flask to mouth
the sudden song of an unknown bird high in a sunlit tree
the unknown fleeting animal without a name
seen in a lifetime only once
the knelt and loving man
whose life is flooded in a womanly tide
the broken glass I kick from the stranger's tire
the face I have never seen
of a friend I do not yet have
those who love me and those who don't
the ton of antiques from the attic of the dead
the child carried by his mom
beaming at me from her shoulder

I am no longer awaiting the world to enter me
I am the world
its sorrows and enchantments

My finger taps impatiently
to the repetition of an ad's annoying return
but the song in my eyes soars
where jets criss-cross in the sunset
and the world beneath is like
the map of life upon my palm
held out to give and take a thousand times
I am not going to stop being
the world when my flesh joins
earth to earth and from my dust
arises whatever ghost sees through
my own eyes for I am that
and more

Ode to a Universal Poet

for Carl Sandburg

America, you tried to contain his starlight
as it blanketed mother and child.

You could not. His imagination was greater
than you are wide. Where you saw water
he saw leaping fish turn into night flowers.
His eyes dove to depths where wisdom
was about to be born. He annointed all
with the forests of his own soul,
causing them to breathe with new lungs
when the old lungs fell to the soil
of distant ages, having been their father,
home from his tireless chores.

America, when you shined your smallish
limelight at his smiling eyes,
they shined their own light
on the myriad ghosts of buffalo herds
as vast as the fields of windy wild grass
they stopped to eat. On sturdy hooves
thundering against the clay of beaten earth,
his thoughts took the wind and made flocks
as vast and loud as canyons full of wings
beating vibrant in the stunned air.

America, the clacking and pinging computers
in a hundred cities could not equal his one mind,
busy like nests of ants and hives of bees,
who in the tongues of insect life turned
their stories into triumpant songs
only life itself would sing, as big
as operas echoing into parlors of
life and death and the infinite soul.

America, there are some who can never
be possessed, never be bought or owned,
or sculpted from the clay of your drab politics
and greed. You may touch his earthy flesh
and still not know that beneath your hand
eternity was stirring, awake and alive
in the furthest reaches of his imagined worlds.

America, you are hungry for your giant saviors, for
the warmth of the kind heart and gentle thought,
which paints the universe onto grains of sand.
That, being both your blessing and your curse,
to ever seek and hope one day to find
that vessel full and overflowing, which,
by dint of its power and virtuous light
lets the souls of many drink drafts of gold
from his endlessly filling tiny cup.

My Secret Sacred World

1.

A mist to be entered when it wills
comes ever so briefly to some
when the wind is strong.

What is it which flies away
upon a thousand beating wings,
like a parent whose love bestowed eternity
and leaves a sweet reminder
that once touched, we are forever transformed?

I have lived a life concerned with death
of others, entranced, seen in glimpses the souls
of those who came in worry and even chaos
deeply felt. Witnessed the coming of their loves,
as mothers, fathers, sisters and brothers. Friends
with simple messages which only they would know
to share. I sat and gleaned whatever was allowed.
I gave those messages my own exactness,
and mimicked the gestures of the ones who spoke
to me alone through my heightened senses and inner ears.
So I have tasted that life purported beyond
the veil of death, giving solace to some
and council to others. Yet mystery
was the courtroom and I a mere dictation clerk.

2.
As an infant I wept mercilessly in every darkness.
I feared dying and death loomed in every shadow.

My brothers wished me dead just so the night
would be at peace. I grew into adolescence
inept at study except what I loved. My mind
evaded spelling, math, and subjects I found dull.

Imagination bloomed in one burst from art
to writing in a single teenage year.
Then late one Spring night while wide awake
that etheric 'I' rose from its body and in a torrent
I could not resist, was pulled toward an open window.
I reached out to stop myself from going through.
My head, and eyes stared straight down the wall
three stories while I felt boneless and made of rubber.
There in front of me was a mammal-like being
with burning red orbs where its eyes should be.
It slithered, with legs held tight to its fur, toward me,
and in one motion I somehow retreated back and awoke.
I never told a soul fearing I was insane.

3.

For twenty years I gave those readings.
Contemplated this twisted gift and finally stopped.

The path of those whose auguries leave a mark
would be enough. The process also has a countenance.
A grander self beyond the self we know. Far wiser,
far richer, than is fathomable by simple self,
which is what I am. The sense of it is far, far greater
than who I am, and yet it calls forth home, and love,
and is a joyful parent whose love is everlasting and
undiminishing. It curls around you, rises within you,
and calms whatever sense of doubt you have ever had.

It is both love and parent, rejoicing and reminding,
that beyond yourself it is a perfect state of life everlasting,
and that you are truly cared for and lifted in its caring arms.

I have tasted but a sip. I know that one day
I will feel its full-blown law as ecstasy and knowing.
I will see my destiny unfold while held within its arms.
I will be made one within its own beating heart.
This and its ultimate sense beyond mere self
is what we are. Incomparable, free as love itself.
But until that day of love anointing, at the appointed
hour of whatever day, I shall continue to learn, to know,
to heal, to cherish, to laugh, to experience and reach for truth.

Acknowledgments

Shelby Keefe: dearest friend, artist; created cover designs for "Empathy Road" and "No Fear."

Eric Mayer: Cover Art for "Empathy Road."

Jody Reid: Oil Portrait of Charles Goldman.

Kathy Link: for her help with formatting "Empathy Road."

Sevan Mercy: For all her personal help, given freely, and so much more than that.

Alison Lechner and Mark Kessinich: amazing best friends when I needed it the most.

Malia Baldry and Nicholaus Westfahl: Coming to aid me as the closest friends imaginable.

Sonja and Chloe Drummond: For demonstrating what loving me truly means.

Bonnie Jonet and Paul Baker, for being two behind-the-scenes friends.

Shawn Stugard: Soul brother, fellow Explorer of Spirit Realms for over some twenty+ years.

Paul Meixner: Eternal brother.

Jordan de la Sierra: For his inspiration to publish this book.

Alex Buck: Best friend in spirit.

Mom: Bess Appelle, and Dad: Louis Goldman without whom I could not exist.

Joel Kellerman: Brother without whom I could not have learned how to forgive.

Daisy Aldan: Life long friend, teacher and influence.

Michael Casares: Poet, Editor - Virgogray press for publisher of "No Fear."